THE HYPOCHONDRIAC
GEORGE DANDIN
SCAPIN

—

Molière

THE HYPOCHONDRIAC
translated by Gerard Murphy

GEORGE DANDIN
~
SCAPIN
translated by Ranjit Bolt

OBERON BOOKS
LONDON

First published in 1998 by Oberon Books Ltd.
(incorporating Absolute Classics),
521 Caledonian Road, London, N7 9RH.
Tel: 0171 607 3637 / Fax: 0171 607 3629

British Library Cataloguing-in-Publication Data
A catalogue record for this book is available from the British Library.

ISBN 1 870259 38 6

Cover design: Andrzej Klimowski

Cover typography: Richard Doust

Printed in Great Britain by Arrowhead Books Ltd., Reading.

CONTENTS

INTRODUCTION

Nicholas Dromgoole

JEAN-BAPTISTE POQUELIN de MOLIERE (1622-1680) was stage-struck most of his life. He was born into a comfortable middle-class merchant's family. In 1631 his father bought the office of upholsterer-in-ordinary to the King, giving him an entrée to the court, and a hereditary post for his eldest son. Molière was well educated, first at the Collège de Clermont, a Jesuit school for the sons of the nobility, gentry and prosperous merchants, then taking a degree in law at Orléans University. At the age of twenty-one he abandoned the upholstery business and his richly upholstered prospects to start a theatre company in Paris, taking the stage-name of Molière. He and his company were a disaster. He stuttered, but fancied himself as a tragedian, a fancy not shared by his audience. Within two years he was in prison for debt, his company having gone bankrupt. His father paid his debts, but far from being repentant, Molière embarked with the members of the Béjart family with whom he had originally started his Illustre Théâtre, on a thirteen-year tour of the provinces, directing his own company for most of the time. It was in these thirteen years, about which we know little, that he learned his trade as an actor, a playwright, a director, a theatre manager, a publicist and a manipulator of men.

In 1658 he gave a command performance before the young King Louis XIV, opening with a tragedy which was not well received, but achieving instant success with a farce written by himself in which he took the leading role. From then on he was installed in Paris at the King's command, originally sharing the Salle du Petit Bourbon with an Italian commedia dell'arte company, directed by the famous Tiberio Fiorillo (Scaramouche). Hostile critics long maintained that many of Molière's best ideas were cribbed from the Italian commedia.

Long before the concept of the Romantic artist, Molière single-mindedly devoted himself to the theatre. He sacrificed family, position, and comfort to belong to it. He lived for it and through it. His amorous affairs seem to have been almost exclusively with fellow thespians, and in the end the theatre killed him. He wrote a leading part for himself in *Le Malade Imaginaire* to accommodate his terrible cough, but at the fourth performance was overcome on stage with a convulsive fit of coughing and died a few hours afterwards.

Molière was undoubtedly one of the great comic actors of his generation – even if he never succeeded, as he longed to do, in a leading tragic role. Yet his real achievements were elsewhere. He transformed the writing of comedy, in the process changing the expectations of his audience. Like most great artists, he was not satisfied with repeating himself. He wanted to innovate and experiment. As a result, he was well ahead of the accepted opinions of his day, almost perpetually involved in controversy, squabbles and sometimes a critical hostility that verged on open warfare. Some of his plays were banned and he aroused the anger and hatred of the medical profession, the clergy and a range of other social groups whom he pilloried and satirised. By the end of his career he had achieved for comedy what another 17th century writer, Racine, achieved for tragedy.

Yet to say this is to use the superior voice of literary hindsight. We can look back and see the 17th century as a whole. When Molière achieved his first triumph in Paris in 1658, attitudes and assumptions were quite otherwise. It was no accident that Molière opened his crucial performance before the King with a tragedy. Tragedy was supreme. He ended and triumphed with a comedy, a comedy close to farce and the clowning of the commedia, and the young King could not stop laughing so of course the rest of the court hooted and applauded too. But none of them would have dreamed of giving that kind of comedy the same status and importance as tragedy. By 1680, when Molière died, his full-length plays, a new kind of comedy, were holding the stage in their own right and were beginning to command a new kind of status. That was Molière's real achievement.

It is sadly necessary at this point to say something about literary criticism in the 17th century. By modern standards it hardly existed at all. There were plenty of people writing animatedly and well about plays, novels and poetry in the 17th century. Yet by our standards they were too blinkered to be thought of as critics. Blinkered because they accepted basic assumptions, and grounded their views firmly upon them, which we can no longer accept.

Firstly, they believed that the purpose of art was to do good, to leave ordinary humans morally better after experiencing it than they were before. Art's job was seen therefore as somehow managing to sweeten the moral pill. And Aristotle had laid down a set of guidelines by which this could be achieved, and to ignore them was to court disaster and failure. Critics therefore asked first what moral improvement resulted from experiencing a particular work, and to what extent it had achieved its ends by following the guidelines laid down in classical antiquity. Since we no longer ask these questions, the answers 17th century critics so copiously produced seem to us curiously dated and irrelevant. But they mattered a great deal at the time. They hampered and made almost impossible any worthwhile discussion of what artists were trying to do. Indeed by modern standards the 17th century is remarkable for the range and splendour of a whole series of artistic creations which it never seemed capable of understanding or appreciating at the time. The tastes of the audience acted as a heavy break on creativity too. Listen to the great Pierre Corneille on how Sophocles could not possibly be a model for a 17th century *Oedipus*.

"I realised that what a previous era had thought miraculous, would be too upsetting for our own. That unlikely and well-spoken part where he pushes the bronze pins into his own eyes and blinds himself, taking up most of Act V, would not suit the tender feelings of the ladies in my audience, and their hostility would spread to others. And as a final remark, there being no love affair, the play is missing what the audience most want. So I have avoided what is offensive, and brought in an affair of the heart between Theseus and Dirce."

One can almost hear a Hollywood producer saying 'This business of putting out his own eyes, I mean that's too gruesome for this kind of classy film, and where's the love interest? You've gotta have love interest. What about this Theseus guy? Couldn't he and Dirce maybe...?'

So one of the great tragedies of ancient Greek theatre had to be sentimentalised almost out of existence to please the ladies. Yet Corneille's *Oedipe* was one of the theatre successes of 1659. Another was *Les Précieuses Ridicules* by Molière. Corneille played with high-sounding rhetoric on themes well within his audience's expectations. Molière was doing something different. He was bringing real life characters, speaking a straightforward, down-to-earth language into the theatre, and making fun of the kind of grand-sounding diction and elaborately worded sentences his audience was so vigorously applauding in their tragedies.

He was doing more than this. Surrounded by busy theatrical activity and all too readily voiced opinions on all sides, he was feeling his way towards a new kind of writing. He needed, of course to take his audience with him. He and his company had royal favour, but they also needed a paying public. Their standard of living depended on their share of the box office takings, and these in Paris could be as precarious as in the provinces.

Royal favour was equally important. Louis XIV was an enlightened despot, an administrative genius who ruled France probably better than it has ever been governed before or since. Like most rulers since the Renaissance, he consciously used the arts to assert his own importance and grandeur. Molière needed the King, not only for royal commissions for court performances, but as a protection against the growing number of social groups Molière's plays infuriated and antagonised. Wisely Molière never made fun of the monarchy. On occasions the King broke all court protocols and had a simple lunch alone with Molière. He enjoyed his company. What would we not give to listen in to such an occasion. The young King, doffing his immense powers, to enjoy the company of his brilliant playwright and actor – *Le Roi s'amuse.* At several crises in his career the staunch support of the King made all the difference to a beleaguered Molière. Despotism is seldom enlightened, but that was what made Louis XIV special. Under the Sun King the arts were warmed and flourished.

It is not only absolute monarchy that separates us off from the 1650s. The mind-set of that French society can now seem bewilderingly alien. What were they doing, all those aristocrats and gentry in their elaborate costumes? The simple answer is – nothing. The whole of French society were labouring long hours to keep them in rich idleness. And this was the last moment in history when nobody questioned the fairness of the system. Because God had ordained the system, and to question the system was to question God, something which, as that awful affair at Loudun was to show, could still provoke punishments medieval in their horrifying severity.

The gap between the aristocrats and the rest had never been greater. They were not only waited on hand and foot, wore different clothes, ate better, lived in fine buildings, kept warm, had time for cultural pursuits – the arts, very much a minority affair. They had dancing masters, who taught them not only to dance, but how to carry themselves in almost every social situation; how to bow, how to enter through a door, how to sit at table, how to sit in a chair and so on. Life was elaborately choreographed. They even walked differently. For riding, and only the rich had horses for their leisure pursuits, they wore long thigh-boots in soft leather. When alighting they rolled the tops of their boots down to their knees. This made walking difficult. They had to turn out their feet, so that the toes of each pointed away from the other foot, and they waddled rather like a duck. In time this became formalised, so that even when not wearing the boots, gentlemen walked as if they were still wearing them to show they were gentlemen and could afford horses, boots and the rest. As a result, aristocrats waddled around pointing the feet outwards. Nobody else did. (This, incidentally, became the basis for what is called 'the turn-out' of the feet in classical ballet which was being codified as an art form by the Royal Academy of Dance set up by Louis XIV.)

All this meant that style, "esprit", became as important to a gentleman as any of his other attributes. He rode, he hawked, he hunted, he learned to fight with a sword, but he also learned to display himself elegantly, to reveal a well-filled mind, to discuss intelligently, to say witty things. It was as important to look good in a lady's salon as on a horse, or attempting to skewer your opponent with a sword. For the first time, mere words could destroy almost as effectively as duelling pistols. Hence the existence of men of breeding and culture in Molière's plays, who say things well, who intend to be witty and are enjoyed as such. That was very much part of his aristocratic court world.

But there was another world. A world he also knew well. The world of his own father. Merchants who worked hard to get on, who spoke a forceful, colloquial language, who had little time for so-called culture and floundered a bit when discussing anything but business. A contemporary called Molière "a constant threat. He takes his eyes and ears everywhere with him!" And what he saw and heard around him Molière introduced into his plays.

Then there was the commedia dell'arte. Drama historians like to banish these lively performers to a footnote or a final paragraph. There are so few surviving texts or indeed written references to them, and drama historians are only really happy arguing about texts. People started writing about commedia dell'arte in the 17th century, but it has a long history which hardly figures at all in textbooks about drama. Alongside the ancient Greek drama festivals, with plenty of texts left for scholars to fasten on, there was another kind of theatre altogether. A mime theatre – a drama which almost dispensed with words. As Athens and then, in turn, the Roman Empire became steadily more cosmopolitan, its audiences an ever wider ethnic mix with a bewildering array of different languages, mime theatre could speak to them all. This mime theatre began in market places, flourished as entertainment at dinner parties, but by the grand days of the Roman Empire was recognised as a powerful art form. In the reign of Augustus mobs clashed in the streets, fighting over the respective merits of the two great mime artists of the day, Bathyllus and Pylades, much as mobs clash in Glasgow over football teams. The plays of Terence and Plautus (Molière is said to have known all the plays of Terence in Latin by heart) owed much to the comic situations of this mime drama.

When the Roman Empire collapsed and Europe was plunged into the anarchy of the Dark Ages, mime drama did not perish. Far from it. In view of the diversity of languages from district to district, it was the only form of theatre that could survive for small, struggling theatrical troupes. We have enough references to know that it was alive and kicking. Attila the Hun, that scourge of Europe, was we read, entertained after dinner with a mime play. When the Dark Ages receded and Europe became steadily more stable and prosperous in the Middle Ages, the Church was very concerned about mime drama. Indeed, most of our knowledge that it existed at all comes from the records of the church's frequent attempts to suppress it. Where there were markets, fairs, pageants, feast days, celebrations of any public kind, there would be a small temporary set-up, charging its audience and offering the clowning and buffoonery of a mime drama. With dialects so dissimilar from place to place, only mime could tour, and small companies had to tour to make a living. Gradually the church established its own drama festivals in the Middle Ages (from which the Oberammergau Passion Play and the York Mystery plays, for example, have happily survived), but there was always an alternative drama "base, common and popular" that everybody knew and felt a bit guilty about enjoying because the church disapproved.

This mime drama kept sufficient characteristics of the Roman mime to make it clear that the continuity was unbroken. They wore masks, they used the same stock characters and their farmyard humour, to use a word that 17th century *précieuses* added to the language, verged on the obscene. Just as Latin remained the common language of the educated right across Europe in the Middle Ages and the early Renaissance, so this mime theatre, going everywhere and seen by so many, established another common language throughout Europe, a language of gesture. We have lost this language, just as surely as we have lost Latin, and we only know about it because specialist art historians have to study it to understand what gestures in paintings from these periods mean. But there was a time when everybody not only recognised it, but doubtless used it. Actors on Shakespeare's stage would step effortlessly into mime routines as they spoke, because the audience understood the mime rather better than the words. Indeed the plays began with an outline of the plot in mime. Nowadays when we go to the nearest equivalent to that mime drama, the ballet, we try to read the programme first so that we have some chance of understanding what is going on. Right up to the 18th century, audiences did the exact opposite. They understood the gestures much better than the words. A fair proportion of Shakespeare's audience would have difficulty reading and writing.

The commedia dell'arte in Paris in the 17th century came close to being a final sophisticated flourish of this long European mime tradition. It was to survive in French boulevard theatre well into the 19th century. Italian players could keep French audiences happy without much of a language barrier. The words were not what mattered. Molière appears to have adored the commedia from his early youth. It must indeed have seemed a marvellous dramatic outlet for someone with a stutter. He took lessons from Tiberio Fiorillo, the famous Scaramouche, in his early days as a would-be actor. When at the King's command Molière's company shared the Salle du Petit Bourbon with the Italian commedia, they were led by Molière's former teacher. He had taught Molière well, so well that Molière brought with him into his new approach for French comedy detailed, specialised and at the same time a wide-ranging knowledge of most of the tricks of the mime trade. He was part of a tradition that led back in unbroken continuity to at least five centuries before the birth of Christ. During that time theatre had learned a thing or two as clown, buffoon and artist succeeded each other. Molière learned what they had learned. He never forgot it and put it to good use.

It is a contribution largely ignored by his friends and only made much of by his enemies. Yet it is essential to a full understanding of his plays. Who pays attention to the fact that his early plays were performed in masks, for example? Or that the sometimes summary seeming endings of his plots would have been masked by a final dance? Dance was an integral part of the commedia dell'arte. It played a much greater part in Molière's plays than modern productions allow. Louis XIV prided himself on his dance ability. Such was the divinity that hedged about a king, we shall never know just how good or bad he really was. But drama historians tend to dismiss the considerable part dance and ballet played in so many Molière productions as being there simply to please the rather strange preoccupations of the young king. This is nonsense.

Dance, social dance was central to the business of being an aristocrat, one of the ways in which men demonstrated their virility, strange as this may seem to a twentieth century which views a male ballet dancer with some suspicion. Theatre dance, or ballet as it was becoming known, was in Molière's time an extension of a language of movement that was an integral part of people's expectations about the theatre. Molière took for granted and used dance as a matter of course, just as he used the movement routines of the clown and buffoon. It was part of his theatrical language. We are the poorer because it is no longer part of ours.

Alongside ten one-act plays, a couple of Molière's plays have two acts, nine have three acts, and twelve have five acts. He was nothing if not versatile, and each play fitted its subject like a glove. There was no padding. W B Yeats talked of "a theatre... joyful, fantastic, extravagant, whimsical, beautiful, resonant and altogether reckless." In his development of the comedy ballet, of which perhaps *Le Bourgeois Gentilhomme* and *Le Malade Imaginaire* (*The Hypochondriac*) represent his finest achievements, Molière did all that Yeats wanted. Those who maintain that the comedy ballet was developed by Molière, largely to satisfy in court performances, the King's love of · music and dance, misunderstand Molière's aims. He was in fact creating a total theatre long before Wagner or Brecht attempted it. For him, song, music and dance were an integral part of a theatre performance, and it is perhaps no accident that his last play, *The Hypochondriac*, made splendid use of them all. By then he had lost favour at court to Lully, who had intrigued against him, and had not only obtained all the rights to any words for which he wrote the music, but also engineered in 1672 a Royal Ordinance reducing the numbers of musicians Molière could use in a production to six singers and twelve instrumentalists, later to be reduced again to two singers and six instrumentalists. It is not surprising that Molière did not ask Lully to compose the music for *The Hypochondriac*, nor was it presented at court at all until well after Molière's death. Charpentier wrote the music, and these song and dance routines must be seen as an integral part of the play that Molière created. The musical interludes both comment on and reinforce the action of the rest of the play, and in this sense Molière was designing a seventeenth century equivalent for the ancient Greek chorus which in its song and dance routines played much the same role. Perhaps it gave Molière a wry satisfaction to be able to use some of the mechanisms of Greek tragedy as he raised the status of comedy in his own time.

The Hypochondriac is rooted in actual experience. Molière was a sick man when he wrote it, and the play about the head of a household preoccupied to the point of obsession with his own health, allowed Molière to make dramatic use when playing the leading role, of his own real and painful cough. At the fourth performance he was taken ill on stage, and although able to finish the evening, he died a few hours later. The central character, Argan shares some characteristics with other major character creations which Molière's plays laid before a startled and delighted public, played it goes without saying, by himself. Startled because in a theatre the audience found themselves confronted by people they could not only believe in but people whose ridiculous traits they recognised only too well. Jourdain the spendthrift, Harpagon's greed, the various snobberies of Alceste, Dandin and Philaminte, Argan's hypochondria, Orgon's exaggerated piety, all obviously evoked an immediate response from the Paris audience.

In a sense each of these outrageous roles share the same variation on a theme. They are all afraid. Afraid of not being in control. They want to be in control of their own households and in the theatre that is a dramatic way of making the point that they desperately need to be in control of themselves. As each play unfolds, the comedy, and their tragedy, is that they lose control. Their very fears help to bring about exactly what they are most afraid of. Even as the audience laughs, they experience that shock of recognition which is theatre's special gift, as the audience recognise their own dilemmas, their own destiny, in the plight of characters on stage they have come imaginatively to accept as real people. In *The Hypochondriac* Argan is obsessed with his own state of health, and attempts to regulate his family affairs around his illness. The play is not so much about hypochondria, as about capitulation to the bizarre demands of the medical profession, the worship of doctors by insecure patients, the medical profession's delusions of grandeur and the social effects on Argan's family as his obsession begins to create havoc in their lives. It may seem to a man obsessed with his own state of health, reasonable to marry off his daughter into the medical profession on which he so desperately relies. To his daughter it does not seem reasonable at all. His calculating second wife, with the dubious lawyer at her side, intends to use her husband's obsession to persuade him to change his will in her favour. She can only do so because his obsession blinds him to reality. Yet his control slips away from him as a result of that same obsession. The very thing he most fears, losing control, is in danger of being caused by his own obsession.

Fortunately the practitioners, the poets and playwrights of the seventeenth century had a better idea of what they were doing than their literary critics. We know what Molière thought about comedy, partly from his *L'Impromptu de Versailles*, a one-act play which shows actors in rehearsal and characters arguing about what they are doing and why. In this Molière played a Marquis who hated Molière, while another actor Brecourt, puts Molière's own defence. Not only was Molière shown arguing against himself, but at the rehearsal he demonstrated to Brecourt how to act Brecourt's own part. Molière was thus playing the role of Brecourt, playing the part of an aristocrat who was putting Molière's case. This is extraordinarily sophisticated drama in its own right, quite apart from the ideas about comedy which fill their conversation. Yet in performance this one-act play is perfectly clear, even simple and straightforward as far as its audience is concerned. Nothing could better demonstrate Molière's skill than this little play which doubtless inspired the Duke of Buckingham's *The Rehearsal*, which in turn produced Sheridan's *The Critic*, to say nothing of Anouilh.

Comedy for Molière lay in anything that was contrary to rationality or common sense. This is a very wide definition. As

W G Moore has pointed out, nobody laughs at Hitler talking of peace when he was preparing for war. Millions of people were to die as a result yet the idea of talking about peace while planning for war is contrary to reason. It is comic. It is also very much Molière's kind of comedy, shot through with hints of tragedy so that even if we laugh, we laugh in despair at the human condition.

Molière offers us no remedies. There is no known remedy for being human. In Molière's plays those who claim to bring remedies, like the medical profession, are all confidence tricksters. They are part of the problem, not its solution. A strong element in humour is the selecting of a scapegoat to laugh at. As we laugh, we reassure ourselves that we belong to the solid majority, and as social animals we need to belong even as we laugh at Molière's unfortunate outcasts and scapegoats. Deep down in our insecurities we know as we watch these outrageous characters struggling in vain, that there, but for a kind destiny, we too might be equally defenceless against a fate we cannot control. Our laughter is a glorious release from fear.

George Dandin, first presented at Versailles in 1668 and later in Paris, was an immediate success. Molière presented three new plays that year whilst still recovering from the first onset of what seems to have been tuberculosis. Of the other two, *Amphitryon* and *L'Avare,* only *L'Avare* failed immediately to please the public. It is easy to see why *George Dandin* succeeded. It seems essentially designed for a bourgeois Paris audience since it pokes delicious fun at the foibles of the aristocracy, although the court apparently enjoyed seeing themselves sent up too. Dandin is a prosperous bourgeois who has married into an aristocratic family and is constantly being snubbed by his father-in-law as he invariably goes wrong in the niceties of social etiquette. His wife intends to have an extra-marital affair and Dandin, desperate to expose her intentions, finds himself cleverly outwitted by her and made to look a fool. There is a crucial moment before she turns the tables when he appears at last to have her in his power and to be able to expose her to her confident and unbelieving father. She begs for understanding and none is forthcoming. It is a key point. He fails her as a man, fails her as a husband, intent only on proving himself in the right and the audience in consequence inclines to her side. The husband as cuckold is a familiar figure from commedia dell'arte and Molière imparts fresh dramatic energy by making him such a believable figure for a bourgeois audience.

Scapin was first performed in Paris at the Palais Royal, the home of Molière's company, in 1671. The plot, which to modern eyes seems fearfully contrived, had a long and illustrious history. It is based on the *Phormio* of Terence, along with other more recent commedia dell'arte versions. Scapin, the son of Brighella, was a familiar figure in the commedia dell'arte canon. Molière, able to recite the plays of Terence by heart in the original Latin, only took from his admired predecessor just what he wanted. The contrivance of the final dénouement, Argante's "Good Heavens! Not *that* bracelet! Why, this is my long-lost daughter, who disappeared when she was four years old!" does creak a bit. It reminds us of the moment when Sheridan satirises this sort of thing in *The Critic* (ironically inspired itself by Molière):

> I am thy father; here's thy mother;
> There thy uncle – those thy first cousins and those
> Are all your near relations!

As Puff declares "There, you see relationships, like murder will out."

Maurice Sand writes "Molière upon being reproached with the follies of Scapin replied 'I saw the public quit *Le Misanthrope* for Scaramouche: I entrusted Scapin with the task of bringing them back again.' "

Of course *Scapin* is an engaging piece of nonsense when compared with some of Molière's major creations, but the public flocked to see it and it has maintained a place in the Molière repertory perhaps because its virtues as an engaging piece of nonsense seem ever more apparent as the years go by. Fathers wishing to arrange a marriage while their offspring have other ideas, were a staple of mime comedy long before Plautus and Terence gave them words to speak on stage. The cunning, untrustworthy servant making rings round his master, has an equally long heritage reaching back well into the days of classical slavery. Molière makes a good deal of fresh fun out of this rather worn material and, such is the irony of history, his comedy routines have now outlived the commedia dell'arte and survived because Molière liked them and incorporated them in his own plays. The servant belabouring his master in a sack, as he pretends to be someone else, must have been the fantasy of many a hard-beaten slave. It still comes alive in Molière's practised hands, and in the original production of the play, Molière himself played Scapin, the clever servant showing off all his commedia expertise no doubt, as he did so. Molière has survived the commedia dell'arte because his comedies still show us people as they undoubtedly are, allowing us to laugh at our discomfiture when confronted with such manifest faults that we undoubtedly share.

So in the end, Molière did have a remedy for the human condition. George Saintsbury has called him "the master of the laugh". And that glorious, if temporary release from fear as we laugh has been his generous legacy to posterity as well as to his own time. He can still make us laugh. It remains a rare gift.

London 1998

(Parts of this introduction have already appeared in the introduction to Ranjit Bolt's translation of *The School For Wives*, Oberon Books, 1997.)

THE HYPOCHONDRIAC

translated by Gerard Murphy

Characters

SHEPHERDESS

LADY

ACTRESS

PUNCHINELLO

MUSICIAN

ACTOR

ARGAN

TOINETTE

ANGELIQUE

BELINE

M. DE BONNEFOIS

CLEANTE

M. DIAFOIRUS

THOMAS

LOUISON

BERALDE

M. FLEURANT

M. PURGON

This adaptation was first performed by the Cambridge
Theatre Company on the 13th of January 1993 at the
Cambridge Arts Theatre with the following cast:

TOINETTE, Kathy Burke

BELINE, Avril Clarke

CLEANTE, James Dreyfus

BERALDE, Kevin Elyot

ANGELIQUE, Debra Gillett

ARGAN, Gerard Murphy

THOMAS, Damon Shaw

PROLOGUE

*The curtain rises to reveal six masked characters on stage: a
SHEPHERDESS, who is in the centre; a LADY; an ACTRESS;
PUNCHINELLO; a MUSICIAN; and an ACTOR. They sing:*

ALL

Your lofty learning is all hot air.
Doctors: you're proud and you're stupid.

SHEPHERDESS

All your big Latin words simply can't get rid
Of my pain, my heartache, my despair.

ALL

Your lofty learning is all hot air.

SHEPHERDESS

I dare not reveal
The tender torture I feel
To that shepherd whose heart I would steal.
But it's to him I'll appeal
For a cure that is real
Only he has the power to heal me.

ALL

Ignorant doctors, away you go
How little you know, how little you care
Your lofty learning is all hot air.

SHEPHERDESS

You boast of your great power
But your medicines and pills
If we took them every hour
Wouldn't cure our ills.

SHEPHERDESS/MEN

You treat decent folk like rabble
With your pompous pointless babble.

SHEPHERDESS/MEN

You hunt together in a pack
Common sense is what you lack.

ALL

Who'd respect you anyway?
Who'd believe a word you say?
Only a booby! Only a jack!
Only a numbskull! Only a hypochondriac!!
Your lofty learning is all hot air.

The curtain falls.

ACT ONE

Scene 1

ARGAN is sitting alone in his room at a table on which he is reckoning up his apothecary's invoices with tokens. He is talking to himself.

ARGAN: Three and two's five, and five's ten and ten's twenty. Three and two's five. "Item: on the twenty-fourth of the month – a mild, preliminary, relaxing colonic irrigation prepared to loosen up, lubricate and refresh sir's bowels." That's what I like about M. Fleurant, my apothecary – his invoices are always so very polite: "prepared to loosen up, lubricate and refresh sir's bowels – thirty sols." What? Being polite isn't everything, M. Fleurant! You've got to be reasonable as well and not try to swindle the sick. Thirty sols for an enema! Until now you've never charged me more than twenty sols and when an apothecary says twenty sols he actually means ten sols, so there, we'll call it ten sols. "Item: on the same day a full penetrative colonic irrigation made up with double catholicon, rhubarb, honey of roses and other ingredients according to the prescription; prepared to wash, scour and thoroughly clean out sir's guts – thirty sols." Excuse me, we'll call that ten sols! "Item: on the evening of the same day a tranquillizing and relaxing potion prepared to calm the liver and help to make sir sleep – thirty-five sols." Well, I won't kick up a fuss about that because I did sleep very soundly. "Item: on the twenty-fifth of the month – a good strong laxative made up with fresh cassia, the best sennapods and other things according to M. Purgon's prescription prepared to purge and excrete sir's bile. Four francs." What! You must be joking M. Fleurant, you're supposed to be kind to the sick. I'm sure M. Purgon didn't instruct you to charge four francs. We'll call it three francs, thank you very much! "Item: on the twenty-sixth of the month, a cathartic douche prepared to dispel sir's wind: thirty sols." We'll call that ten sols, M. Fleurant. "Item: a preventative tonic made up of twelve grains of dried cow's stomach, lemon cordial, pomegranate and other things according to the prescription – five francs." Be gentle, M. Fleurant, please be gentle; if you carry on like this I won't be able to afford to be sick. I think you ought to be happy with four francs. Good! Now let me see – this month I've taken: One, two, three, four, five, six, seven, eight medicaments and I've had: One, two, three, four, five, six, seven, eight, nine, ten, eleven, twelve enemas and last month I took twelve medicaments and had twenty enemas. That's why I've felt worse this month than I did last month. I must have a word with M. Purgon so that he can do something about it. Come along! Will someone please clear these things away. Is there no-one there? It doesn't matter what I say, I'm always left alone. No-one pays any attention to me. (*He rings a bell to call his servants.*) They can't hear – my bell mustn't be big enough. (*D'ring, d'ring, d'ring.*) They're all deaf. Toinette! (*D'ring, d'ring, d'ring.*) It's no use. (*D'ring, d'ring, d'ring.*) They're all deaf. Toinette! (*D'ring, d'ring, d'ring.*) You'd think I wasn't ringing at all. Bitch! Whore! (*D'ring, d'ring d'ring.*) I'm losing my temper! (*He stops ringing the bell and shout*s.) D'ring, d'ring, d'ring! Go to hell, witch! How can they leave a poor invalid all alone like this. D'ring, d'ring, d'ring – it's awful. D'ring, d'ring, d'ring – oh God, they'll leave me here to die. D'ring, d'ring, d'ring!

Scene 2

TOINETTE: (*Coming into the room.*) I'm coming!

ARGAN: You bitch!...You witch!

TOINETTE: (*Pretending that she's banged her head.*) You're so
   bloody impatient. You're always making people rush
   about and I've banged my head on the edge of a shutter.

ARGAN: (*Furious.*) You liar...

TOINETTE: (*Interrupting to stop him from shouting.*) Ahhh!

ARGAN: It's been...

TOINETTE: Ahhh!

ARGAN: It's been an hour...

TOINETTE: Ahhh!

ARGAN: Since you left me...

TOINETTE: Ahhhhhh!

ARGAN: Will you shut up, you whore, so that I can shout
   at you.

TOINETTE: Oh yes, very good, very nice, charming,
   after what I've done to myself.

ARGAN: I'm hurting my throat because of you, you witch!

TOINETTE: And you made me crack my skull. One good
   turn deserves another. I think we're quits now, thank
   you very much.

ARGAN: What! You whore...

TOINETTE: If you shout, I'll cry.

ARGAN: Leaving me on my own like that, you liar...

TOINETTE: (*Still interrupting him.*) Ahhh!

ARGAN: You bitch, you want...

TOINETTE: Ahhhh!

ARGAN: Are you not even going to let me have the
   pleasure of shouting at you?

TOINETTE: Shout as much as you like, I don't care.

ARGAN: I can't shout at you, you silly bitch, if you keep interrupting me.

TOINETTE: I told you, if you're going to shout, I'm going to cry; fair's fair. Ahhhhh!

ARGAN: All right, all right. I give up! I give up! Get rid of all this stuff, you whore. (*He gets out of his chair.*) Did the enema that I had today work well?

TOINETTE: Your enema?

ARGAN: Yes! Have I excreted much bile?

TOINETTE: I don't know. I don't get involved in that sort of thing. That's for M. Fleurant to stick his nose into. That's how he earns his money.

ARGAN: Make sure they bring up some boiling water for my next irrigation. I must have another one soon.

TOINETTE: That M. Fleurant and M. Purgon really enjoy themselves at your expense. They're bleeding you dry. I would like to ask them to tell me what exactly is wrong with you that you have to take so many remedies.

ARGAN: Keep quiet, you nincompoop, you don't understand anything about medicine. Go and bring Angelique here. I've something to tell her.

TOINETTE: She's coming by herself – she must have read your mind.

ANGELIQUE enters.

Scene 3

ARGAN: Come over here, Angelique, you couldn't have come at a better time. I want to talk to you.

ANGELIQUE: Well, I'm here. What do you want to tell me?

ARGAN: (*Running to the toilet.*) Wait here. Give me my stick. I'll be back in a minute.

TOINETTE: (*Making fun of him.*) Go quickly, sir, go quickly. That M. Fleurant keeps you on the run.

ARGAN leaves. Farting noises come from ARGAN's rooms.

He certainly gives your "lower regions" plenty of exercise.

Scene 4

ANGELIQUE: (*Looks yearningly and says confidentially.*) Toinette?

TOINETTE: What?

ANGELIQUE: Look at me.

TOINETTE: All right! I'm looking at you.

ANGELIQUE: Toinette!

TOINETTE: What's all this "Toinette"?

ANGELIQUE: Can't you guess what I want to talk about?

TOINETTE: Oh, I think I might be able to. It's about your boyfriend, isn't it? That's the only thing we've talked about for the last six days. You're miserable when you're not talking about him.

ANGELIQUE: If you knew that then why didn't you talk about first to save me the embarrassment of having to mention him to you again?

TOINETTE: You didn't give me a chance.

ANGELIQUE: I know. It's terrible. I just can't stop talking about him and you know I love telling you all my secrets. Tell me Toinette, do you think I'm stupid to feel the way I do about him?

TOINETTE: Not a bit.

ANGELIQUE: Is it wrong to become so obsessed with him?

TOINETTE: I never said it was.

ANGELIQUE: Do you think I should just ignore all the sweet and passionate things he says to me?

TOINETTE: God forbid.

ANGELIQUE: Don't you think that it's as if Heaven or the Fates, against all the odds, must have arranged for us to meet each other?

TOINETTE: Yes.

ANGELIQUE: Don't you think the way he leapt to my defence, without even knowing me, was the action of a true gentleman?

TOINETTE: Yes.

ANGELIQUE: No-one could have been more chivalrous?

TOINETTE: No-one.

ANGELIQUE: No-one could have been more charming?

TOINETTE: No-one could!

ANGELIQUE: Don't you think that he's really good-looking?

TOINETTE: Definitely.

ANGELIQUE: Hasn't he got a wonderful personality?

TOINETTE: He has.

ANGELIQUE: Isn't everything he says and everything he does just sublime?

TOINETTE: Sublime.

ANGELIQUE: No-one could begin to imagine the kind of sexy things he says to me.

TOINETTE: I'm sure they couldn't.

ANGELIQUE: Isn't it dreadful that I'm locked up like this? Isn't it a crime that we are prevented from sharing our love, especially when our love was planned in Heaven?

TOINETTE: You have a point.

ANGELIQUE: Tell me, my dear Toinette, do you really think that he loves me as much as he says he does?

TOINETTE: Well, when it comes to love you've got to be careful. It's hard to tell the difference between the libertine and the lover. I've known some good play actors in both roles, believe me.

ANGELIQUE: What are you trying to say Toinette? Do you think he's just been telling me a pack of lies?

TOINETTE: All will soon be revealed. Didn't he write you a letter yesterday saying that he was going to ask for your hand in marriage? That'll be the test – either he will or he won't.

ANGELIQUE: If he's been lying to me Toinette, I swear I'll never believe another man again as long as I live.

TOINETTE: Look, your father's coming back.

ARGAN enters.

Scene 5

ARGAN: (*Sitting down in his chair.*) There you are, my child. Now, I have a bit of unexpected news for you. Someone has asked for your hand in marriage. What's this? You're laughing? Oh yes, it's a wonderful word "marriage". I suppose it's the word that every young girl longs to hear. Ah, l'amour, l'amour. Well, from the look on your face I don't have to ask if you'd like to be married.

ANGELIQUE: I'll do whatever you want me to do, father.

ARGAN: How wonderful to have such an obedient daughter. Well, it's all arranged. I've promised your hand in marriage.

ANGELIQUE: I will blindly obey your wishes, father.

ARGAN: Your step-mother wanted me to send you and your little sister to a convent. She's always wanted that.

TOINETTE: She would.

ARGAN: At first she wouldn't agree to the marriage but I managed to persuade her and now I've given my word.

ANGELIQUE: Oh father, you're so kind. Thank you.

TOINETTE: I must say that I'm delighted. It's the most sensible thing you've ever done in your whole life!

ARGAN: I've never seen the boy but they tell me that I'll be pleased with him and I hope he'll please you too.

ANGELIQUE: Oh yes he will.

ARGAN: How do you know? Have you seen him?

ANGELIQUE: Since you've agreed to our marriage I can now tell you everything. We met, by chance, six days ago, fell in love at first sight and now he's asked you for my hand in marriage.

ARGAN: They didn't tell me that but I'm very glad. I like a happy ending. They say that he's a good-looking young man.

ANGELIQUE: Yes father.

ARGAN: Handsome.

ANGELIQUE: Oh yes.

ARGAN: A nice person.

ANGELIQUE: Very nice.

ARGAN: A lovely face.

ANGELIQUE: Really lovely!

ARGAN: Sensible and well mannered.

ANGELIQUE: He is.

ARGAN: Honourable.

ANGELIQUE: The most honourable man in the world.

ARGAN: Good at Latin and Greek.

ANGELIQUE: Is he? I don't know anything about that.

ARGAN: And in three day he'll be a qualified doctor.

ANGELIQUE: A doctor?

ARGAN: Yes. Didn't he tell you that?

ANGELIQUE: No. Who told you?

ARGAN: M. Purgon.

ANGELIQUE: M. Purgon! Does he know him?

ARGAN: Don't be silly. Of course he knows him. He ought to know his own nephew.

ANGELIQUE: Cleante is M. Purgon's nephew?

ARGAN: What do you mean "Cleante"? I'm talking about the man who has asked for your hand in marriage.

ANGELIQUE: Yes, I know.

ARGAN: Well! It's M. Purgon's nephew, the son of his brother-in-law, M. Diafoirus, the doctor, and he's called Thomas, Thomas Diafoirus, not Cleante. This morning M. Purgon, M. Fleurant and I arranged the marriage and tomorrow the young man is being brought over here by his father. What's wrong? Why are you looking at me like that? Say something!

ANGELIQUE: What can I say? I've just realised you've been talking about one person and I've been thinking about someone completely different.

ANGELIQUE exits.

TOINETTE: Oh really sir, how could you have started such a ludicrous comedy? You've got money to burn and you want to marry your daughter to a doctor.

ARGAN: Yes I do! Is it any of your business, you cheeky little whore?

TOINETTE: Take it easy, sir. You're always calling people names. Can't we have a reasonable conversation without flying off the handle? Come on, let's have a rational discussion. Please tell me why you have arranged this marriage?

ARGAN: I have arranged this marriage because, as you know, I am not well. I am sick and I would like to have a son-in-law from a medical family to give me advice about my illnesses. I want relatives who can supply me with medicines when I require them, give me consultations when I want them, and issue me with prescriptions when I need them.

TOINETTE: Fine, now we know the reason. I must say, it's very nice to hear you talk to me about it calmly. Please cross your heart sir, and answer this question honestly: are you really sick?

ARGAN: You stupid whore! Am I really sick? Am I really sick? You cheeky...! Am I really sick?

TOINETTE: All right, all right! You're really sick! You're really sick! Let's not have a fight about it. I agree! You're really very sick. Very, very sick. Much sicker than you think. But your daughter should marry for herself. She's not sick. She doesn't need a doctor.

ARGAN: But I need a doctor. I need a doctor and if she was a real daughter, she would be happy to marry anyone who might help to improve her father's health.

TOINETTE: Would you like me to give you a little friendly advice, sir?

ARGAN: What advice?

TOINETTE: Forget about this marriage.

ARGAN: Why?

TOINETTE: Why? You want me to tell you "why"? Because your daughter will never agree to it.

ARGAN: My daughter will never agree to it?

TOINETTE: No! She'll have nothing to do with M. Diafoirus or with Thomas Diafoirus or with any other person who might be called Diafoirus.

ARGAN: Let me explain a few things. There are certain advantages to this marriage you haven't even thought of. One: M. Diafoirus has only the one son, he'll leave everything to him; Two: M. Purgon has no family – he approves of this marriage and he'll leave everything to his nephew and we know the interest on his capital comes to, at least, eight thousand francs a year.

TOINETTE: He must have killed off a lot of patients to become so rich.

ARGAN: Eight thousand francs a year from the uncle plus what the father's worth – it's a great deal of money!

TOINETTE: That's true, sir, but I must come back to the point. Just between ourselves let me advise you to pick another husband for your daughter. Let me tell you here and now that she won't ever become Madame Diafoirus.

ARGAN: Oh yes she will! She will!

TOINETTE: Don't say that.

ARGAN: What do you mean "don't say that"?

TOINETTE: Just don't.

ARGAN: Why not?

TOINETTE: If anyone hears you talking like that they'll
   say you've gone mad.

ARGAN: They can say whatever they like, but she'll
   marry the man that I have chosen for her.

TOINETTE: She won't.

ARGAN: I'll make her.

TOINETTE: She won't do it.

ARGAN: She will – or else I'll put her in a convent!

TOINETTE: You will?

ARGAN: I will.

TOINETTE: Good!

ARGAN: What do you mean "good"?

TOINETTE: You'll never put her in a convent.

ARGAN: I'll never put her in a convent?

TOINETTE: No.

ARGAN: No?

TOINETTE: No.

ARGAN: This must be some kind of joke. Why won't I put
   my daughter into a convent if I want to?

TOINETTE: You won't.

ARGAN: And who'll stop me?

TOINETTE: You will.

ARGAN: I will?

TOINETTE: Yes, you won't have the heart!

ARGAN: I will.

TOINETTE: Don't kid yourself.

ARGAN: I'm not kidding myself.

TOINETTE: Your own fatherly feelings will stop you.

ARGAN: They will not stop me.

TOINETTE: A few tears, arms around your neck, a few tender words: "my own dear darling daddy" – all that sort of thing will completely melt your heart.

ARGAN: Oh no it won't.

TOINETTE: Oh yes it will!

ARGAN: I'm telling you that it won't affect me!

TOINETTE: Bullshit!

ARGAN: How dare you say "bullshit" to me.

TOINETTE: Dear God, I know you. Beneath this ridiculous exterior you're a really good person.

ARGAN: I am not a really good person! I can be a really bad person when I want to be.

TOINETTE: Take it easy, sir, don't forget you're a sick man.

ARGAN: I unconditionally command my daughter to marry the man that I have chosen for her.

TOINETTE: And I unconditionally forbid her to marry him.

ARGAN: What is the world coming to when a whore of a servant dares to speak like that in front of her master?

TOINETTE: When a master doesn't know what he's doing it's a good servant's duty to rap him over the knuckles.

ARGAN: (*Running after TOINETTE.*) You checky tart. I'll beat the shit out of you.

TOINETTE: (*Avoiding him.*) It's my duty to stop you making a fool of yourself sir.

ARGAN: (*Very angry, runs round his chair after TOINETTE, waving his stick.*) Come here, come here! I'll teach you not to speak to me like that!

TOINETTE: (*Running, avoiding him on the other side of the chair.*) I'm only doing my duty. I won't let you do anything stupid.

ARGAN: Bitch!

TOINETTE: I will never allow this marriage.

ARGAN: Trollop!

TOINETTE: I will never let her marry Thomas Diafoirus.

ARGAN: Witch!

TOINETTE: She'll obey me, she won't listen to you.

ARGAN: Angelique! (*ANGELIQUE re-enters.*) Grab hold of that bitch for me.

ANGELIQUE: Daddy, please don't make yourself ill.

ARGAN: Stop her! I'm warning you!

TOINETTE: If she obeys you – I'm going to cut her out of my will. She won't get a penny from me.

TOINETTE and ANGELIQUE exeunt.

ARGAN: (*Exhausted, flings himself into his chair – alone.*) Oh, I'm finished. I'm going to die – all this will definitely kill me!

Scene 6

BELINE enters.

ARGAN: Come here, my darling wife, come here.

BELINE: What's wrong, my precious husband, what's wrong?

ARGAN: Oh help me, please!

BELINE: What's the matter with my little Bubba?

ARGAN: Oh Mimsy!

BELINE: My little pet.

ARGAN: They're going to make me have a haemorrhage.

BELINE: There, there, my brave little soldier, tell Mimsy all about it.

ARGAN: Your friend, that whore Toinette, is being very nasty to me.

BELINE: Now, now, don't get over-excited.

ARGAN: She's making me get over-excited, Mimsy.

BELINE: Take it easy, my little Bubba!

ARGAN: For the last hour she's been doing exactly the opposite to what I tell her to do.

BELINE: There, there, now, gently, gently.

ARGAN: She even had the nerve to tell me that I'm not really sick.

BELINE: She's a bad girl.

ARGAN: You know the truth, my precious heart, you know the truth.

BELINE: Oh yes I do, and she's wrong, sweetheart, she's wrong.

ARGAN: Oh my love, I know that she's trying to kill me.

BELINE: There, there. Ssh! Ssh!

ARGAN: She's got a lot to answer for.

BELINE: Don't let yourself get so upset.

ARGAN: How many times have I told you to get rid of her?

BELINE: Heavens above, Bubba, all servants, male and female, have their shortcomings! We've got to put up

with their weak points because of their good points. This
one is neat, careful, hard-working and above all, she is
loyal and you know that nowadays one can't be too
careful about the sort of people one employs. Toinette!

TOINETTE re-enters.

Come here!

TOINETTE: Madam.

BELINE: Why have you upset my husband?

TOINETTE: (*Very sweetly.*) Me madam? I'm sorry but
I don't know what you're talking about. I'm always
trying to make sir happy.

ARGAN: Liar!

TOINETTE: He announced that he was going to marry
his daughter to M. Diafoirus' son and I only said that
although it was clearly a good match, he'd be better off
sending her to a convent.

BELINE: There's no harm in that, darling. In fact, I agree
with her.

ARGAN: Don't believe her, my love. Don't believe a
word she says. She's an evil cow and she's always
insulting me.

BELINE: All right. All right. Come along now pet, pull
yourself together. Listen to me, Toinette. If you ever
again upset my husband, you're fired. Now get me his
fur blanket and his pillows so that I can make him
comfortable in his chair. What do you look like, darling?
Pull your cap right down over your ears. Don't let the
nasty night air get into your ears or you'll catch a cold.

ARGAN: Thank you for looking after me, Mimsy.

BELINE: (*Plumping the pillows as she arranges them around
ARGAN.*) Lift up and let me put this one underneath you.

This one on one side. This one on the other side. This one for your back. This one for your head.

TOINETTE: (*Shoves a pillow on his face and runs out.*) And this one to keep out the nasty night air.

ARGAN: (*Gets up angrily throwing all the pillows after TOINETTE.*) Whore! I know! You want to suffocate me!

BELINE: There, there. What's the matter now?

ARGAN: (*Throws himself into his chair, out of breath.*) Ah! Ahh! Ahhh! Ahhhh! I can't take much more of this.

BELINE: Why do you let yourself get so hysterical. She means well.

ARGAN: You don't know, my poor innocent darling, just how evil she is. She's made me feel really awful and I know it's going to take at least eight doses of medicine and at least twelve enemas to make me feel better.

BELINE: There, there, my dearest love, do try to calm down a little.

ARGAN: You are my only crumb of comfort, Mimsy.

BELINE: My poor little Bubba.

ARGAN: Sweetheart, to thank you for loving me so much, I want to make my will.

BELINE: Oh my little pet, please don't talk to me about things like that. I can't even bear to think about such things. The very word "will" makes me shiver.

ARGAN: I've told you to speak to the notary about it.

BELINE: I have. He's here. I brought him with me.

ARGAN: Bring him in, my love, bring him in.

BELINE: Oh my darling, when a woman loves her husband as much as I love you, she's in no state to deal with things like this.

She gets M. DE BONNEFOIS.

Scene 7

ARGAN: Come in M. de Bonnefois, come in. Please sit down. My wife tells me you are an honest man, sir, and one of her best friends, so I've instructed her to speak to you about a will that I wish to make.

BELINE: Oh God, I simply can't begin to talk about this kind of thing.

M. DE BONNEFOIS: She's already told me what you'd like, sir. About your plans for her. It is my duty, however, to inform you you can't bequeath anything to your wife.

ARGAN: Why not?

M. DE BONNEFOIS: The local law forbids it. Such a will would be null and void here in Paris. Local law is riddled with obscure customs and practices that override the laws of the land. Every city, every district, every region has its own legal traditions, its own peculiar set of bye-laws. The laws concerning wills are very complicated indeed. For example, if one were to try to make over one's estate to one's partner, the legacy would be invalid if there was a child of the marriage, or indeed of a previous marriage, in existence when the testator was declared deceased. Of course, if you lived south of the Loire, things would be different. But, in Paris, the most effective way wealth can pass between a married couple is by means of a deed of gift drawn up by mutual consent while both parties are still alive.

ARGAN: Are you trying to tell me that a man can't leave his estate to his wife who loves him, who cherishes him, who dotes on him? I'm going to have to speak to my lawyer to find out what I can do.

M. DE BONNEFOIS: There's no point in going to a lawyer, sir. They are usually very strict about such things and often consider it a crime if one even attempts to circumvent the law. Lawyers create problems and are completely insensitive to human feelings. There are other kinds of advisors who can be much more helpful, who can get round the law without any fuss, who make things happen. Who can smooth out problems and find clever ways to evade local law. Where would we be without them?

ARGAN: My wife, sir, was right when she said you were both clever and honest. Please tell me how I can make sure that everything goes to her and not to my children.

M. DE BONNEFOIS: Let's see. What can you do? For a start, you could secretly make out a legal will in favour of one of your wife's best friends, leaving as much as you can to him and then, after your death, he will of course give it all to her. At the same time, you could make out a large number of bonds favouring various creditors who, for your wife's sake, have allowed their names to be used. They, in turn, will give her papers stating the money is, in fact, hers. Of course, while you are still alive you should also give her cash or promissory notes made payable to the bearer.

BELINE: Dear God, you shouldn't be troubled with this sort of thing. If you were to die, Bubba, I would have nothing left to live for.

ARGAN: Oh Mimsy!

BELINE: Yes, my pet, if I were so cursed as to lose you I wouldn't want to go on living.

ARGAN: My dear, sweet wife.

BELINE: Life would mean nothing to me.

ARGAN: My dearest love.

BELINE: I swear that I will follow you beyond the grave to prove how much I love you.

ARGAN: Mimsy, you are breaking my heart. Please be comforted.

M. DE BONNEFOIS: Thankfully, there's no need for all this crying yet madame. Your husband's still alive.

BELINE: Oh sir, you can't imagine what it's like to have a husband that you love so very much.

ARGAN: When I do come to die, my only regret will be that I didn't have a child by you. M. Purgon assured me that he would see to it for me.

M. DE BONNEFOIS: He probably will. There's still time.

ARGAN: My will must be made in exactly the way this gentleman has explained to us my love. Meanwhile I will give you twenty thousand francs in gold, that I have kept behind the panelling in my private chamber and I'll also give you two promissory notes that I'm owed, one from M. Damon and one from M. Geronte. I'll make them payable to the bearer.

BELINE: No, no! I really don't want any of it. By the way, how much did you say was in your private chamber?

ARGAN: Twenty thousand francs, my love.

BELINE: Please don't talk to me about money. Incidentally, how much are the promissory notes worth?

ARGAN: One's worth four thousand francs, my dear, the other's worth six thousand.

BELINE: All the wealth in the whole world is worth nothing to me compared with you my love.

M. DE BONNEFOIS: Shall we draw up the will?

ARGAN: Oh yes, indeed sir. I think we'd all be more comfortable in my private little study. Please help me there my dear.

BELINE: My poor, precious little Bubba, come along with me.

Exeunt.

Scene 8

TOINETTE and ANGELIQUE enter.

TOINETTE: They're with a notary and I heard them talking about a will. Your stepmother's no dozer and I'm certain that she's pushing your father into some plot that won't do you any good at all.

ANGELIQUE: Let him throw away his money any way he wants to, just so long as he doesn't throw away my heart. Can't you see that all of this is killing me? Oh, Toinette, now when I need you most, please don't desert me.

TOINETTE: Me desert you? I'd rather die! Your stepmother tells me all her secrets and would like me to help her but I've never liked her. I've always been on your side. Leave everything to me. To be of most use I'm going to have to hide my concern for you and pretend to agree with everything they say and do.

ANGELIQUE: Please try to warn Cleante about this marriage they've arranged.

TOINETTE: I know who can do that for us; that old usurer, my lover, Punchinello! It'll cost me a whole lot of honeyed words but I don't mind because it's for you. It's too late to do anything tonight but the first thing tomorrow morning I'll send someone to find him and he'll be thrilled to...

BELINE: (*Offstage.*) Toinette!

TOINETTE: They're calling me. Goodnight. Trust me...

Curtain.

INTERLUDE

The curtain rises. PUNCHINELLO comes on to the stage with a musician who carries a stringed instrument. PUNCHINELLO talks to the audience.

PUNCHINELLO: Oh love, love, love, love! Poor me! Poor Punchinello. Look at me! I must be possessed or it's just possible that I've gone mad. Anyway, it's pathetic. I keep wasting my time dressing up in silly clothes, singing daft songs and trying to make stupid speeches – like this one. I wasn't cut out for this sort of thing but I don't seem to care. I don't do any work – everything's gone to wrack and ruin; I don't eat; I don't drink – well, not enough; and I can't get to sleep at night; and all for what? For a dragon, an absolute dragon, an out and out she-devil who looks down her nose at me and makes fun of everything I try to say to her. "Oh love, love, love, love!" Yes, I know; you don't have to tell me – it's pitiful, but there's no point in trying to be logical about it. When you're courting someone you go a bit soft in the head – it's as simple as that. I don't know why, but it happens – even at my age it happens. I've been around long enough to know that love isn't the greatest thing in the world. Once you've got it it's not all it's cracked up to be but I still can't help myself. What can I do? It's not always possible to be wise when you want to be and older men can be smitten as badly as the young ones – believe me! Anyway as you can see, I'm well and truly smitten and I've come here today looking like a fool and feeling like an even bigger one to try to sweeten my intended's stony heart with a serenade. Yes, I'm afraid it's come to this – a serenade. I've even brought my own accompanist.

The MUSICIAN bows to the audience.

I can't count the number of nights I've stood looking like a half-wit in the freezing cold, singing love songs to locked doors and bolted windows but tonight it will be different. Tonight she's going to listen to me. Come gentle night, come loving black-browed night. Carry my heartfelt lamentations right into the bed of my inflexible mistress.

MUSICIAN plays a chord very badly.

I thought you said you could play that thing.

MUSICIAN plays another chord badly.

Is this some kind of joke?

MUSICIAN plays another chord badly.

When you took this job you said you were an accomplished musician.

MUSICIAN: I am.

PUNCHINELLO: It doesn't sound like it.

MUSICIAN: The guitar is not my instrument.

PUNCHINELLO: What is your instrument?

MUSICIAN: The glockenspiel.

PUNCHINELLO: The glockenspiel?

MUSICIAN: Yes, and when I have to I can also play the bagpipes.

PUNCHINELLO: Oh well, faint heart never made love to a heifer. Let's get on with it.

Sings.

> All through the dark eternal night.
> All through the day's incessant light

I love you, I adore you
I worship at your shrine.
Ease my distress, say "yes, you will be mine"
If you say "no", then by all the powers divine
I'll die for you;
Unfeeling vixen at your feet I'll fall, supine.
What hope is left for my poor aching heart
If you and I must always be apart.
Just let me know that one day you may care
Or kill me now and end this bleak despair.
All through the dark eternal night.
All through the day's incessant light
I love you, I adore you
I worship at your shrine.
Ease my distress, say "yes, you will be mine"
If you say "no", then by all the powers divine
I'll die for you;
Unfeeling vixen at your feet I'll fall, supine.

The ACTRESS enters making a lot of noise with a tambourine.

ACTRESS: My landlady says that if you don't stop this caterwauling she will send her servant out to throw a bucket of water over you!

PUNCHINELLO: (*To the MUSICIAN.*) It's all your fault! (*To the ACTRESS.*) Will she not grant me even one word?

ACTRESS: The only words she has for you are "*go away*". Now please let us get some sleep. You're the third lot that have come round serenading her this evening.

PUNCHINELLO: You mean, she has other admirers.

ACTRESS: Of course she has.

PUNCHINELLO: How many?

ACTRESS: Lots of men find her attractive. I couldn't begin to count them.

PUNCHINELLO: I'm shocked. She must be a loose woman.

ACTRESS: No, she is not! She pays no attention to any of them and that includes you. Now please *go away*.

PUNCHINELLO: I'm going, I'm going. I don't want to stand here and be insulted by jades and harlots. (*To the MUSICIAN.*) Come on, let's go back to your house. You can play me a tune on your bagpipes.

PUNCHINELLO and the MUSICIAN exeunt.

ACTRESS: (*Shouting offstage.*) They've gone.

LADY enters.

LADY: Well done my dear.

ACTRESS: Are you really not interested in him at all?

LADY: Not a bit.

ACTRESS: Don't you want to have a lover? Don't you want to be happy?

LADY: My dear girl, those two things rarely exist side by side. Most men use us women merely to make a conquest. Women have two choices. We can submit to the market and let ourselves be bought and sold or we can be self-sufficient. I've chosen to be strong and will present myself to the world as any man's equal.

Sings.

> All you heartsick hopefuls
> With your cheating looks
> Your delusive longings
> You're a pack of crooks.
> Little boy lovers
> With your shifty eyes
> Your dubious advances

You do not have what satisfies.
Boast about your honesty
Beg to win my trust
None of that can fool me
All you know about is lust.
I'm a woman of the world
My life has not been sad
For experience has taught me
That any lady who believes a man is mad.

Curtain falls.

ACT TWO

Scene 1

Next morning.

TOINETTE: What do you want sir?

CLEANTE: What do I want?

TOINETTE: Oh, it's you! What a surprise! What are you doing here?

CLEANTE: I've come to know my fate. I want to speak privately with Angelique to find out how she feels about me. I want to ask her what she proposes to do about this disastrous marriage that I've been warned about.

TOINETTE: I'm sure you do! But you mustn't talk as bluntly as that to Angelique. Be subtle. I don't have to tell you that she's watched all the time, not allowed to go out and forbidden to speak to anyone. It was only because she was with an old aunt we were ever allowed to go to that play where your little romance first blossomed.

CLEANTE: I know. That's why I've come in disguise. Don't think of me as Cleante, her lover. Think of me as her music master. Her real teacher is a friend of mine and he's let me come to give her a lesson in his place.

TOINETTE: Her father's coming. Stand over there and let me tell him that you're here.

Scene 2

ARGAN enters.

ARGAN: M. Purgon has instructed me to walk backwards and forwards twelve times every morning in my room but I forgot to ask him if he meant up and down, longitudinally or side to side, latitudinally.

TOINETTE: Sir, there's a...

ARGAN: Speak quietly, you little trollop. You're giving me a splitting headache. You seem to forget that no-one should ever speak so loudly to a sick man.

TOINETTE: Sir, I wanted to tell you...

ARGAN: Speak quietly, I said.

TOINETTE: Sir... (*She pretends to speak.*)

ARGAN: What?

TOINETTE: I just wanted to say... (*She pretends to speak.*)

ARGAN: What are you saying?

TOINETTE: (*Loudly.*) There's a man who wants to speak to you.

ARGAN: Bring him here.

TOINETTE signals for CLEANTE to come forward.

CLEANTE: Sir...

TOINETTE: (*Mockingly.*) Don't speak so loudly in case you give him a splitting headache.

CLEANTE: Sir, I'm delighted you're up and about and I'm pleased to see you're feeling better!

TOINETTE: (*Pretending to be angry.*) What do you mean "feeling better"? That's a downright lie! Sir is always sick.

CLEANTE: I'd heard that he was feeling better and I thought that he was looking rather well.

TOINETTE: What do you mean "looking rather well"? He looks terrible. I can't imagine who could've had the impertinence to suggest that he was "feeling better". He has never been worse.

ARGAN: She is absolutely right.

TOINETTE: Oh, I know that he walks, sleeps, eats and drinks just like everyone else but that doesn't mean that he isn't a very very sick man.

ARGAN: That's true.

CLEANTE: I'm really sorry, sir. Allow me to explain why I'm here. I've come as a substitute for your daughter's singing teacher. He's had to go to the country for a few days and because I'm a close friend he asked me to take his place and continue the lessons in case your daughter should forget what she's already learned.

ARGAN: Very good. Call Angelique.

TOINETTE: I think it might be better sir, to take the gentleman to her room.

ARGAN: No, bring her here.

TOINETTE: He won't be able to give her a proper lesson if they don't have privacy.

ARGAN: Of course he will!

TOINETTE: The noise might make you feel light-headed sir and in your condition you shouldn't be upset in any way or you'll get one of your migraines.

ARGAN: Not at all. I love music and I'll be only too delighted to... Ah, here she is. (*ANGELIQUE enters.*) Go and see if my wife is dressed yet.

TOINETTE exits.

Scene 3

ARGAN: Come on in Angelique. Your music teacher's had to go to the country but he's sent this gentleman to give you your lesson.

ANGELIQUE: Good heavens.

ARGAN: What's wrong? Why are you so surprised?

ANGELIQUE: It's just...

ARGAN: What is it? What's happened to you?

ANGELIQUE: I've just had the most extraordinary déjà-vu.

ARGAN: What do you mean?

ANGELIQUE: Last night I dreamed that I was in dreadful trouble and in the dream someone who looked just like this gentleman came to me. I asked for his help and he gave it. He rescued me. It's a bit of a shock to suddenly see here, in the house, the person who's been in my mind all night.

CLEANTE: I am happy to be in your thoughts, waking or sleeping. It would be my pleasure to be considered worthy to rescue you from any trouble you might be in. To tell the truth there isn't anything that I wouldn't do...

TOINETTE comes running in.

Scene 4

TOINETTE: (*Defensively.*) Forgive me, sir, forgive me. I agree with you. I take back everything I said yesterday. M. Diafoirus senior and young Master Diafoirus have come to visit you. You're going to have a fantastic son-in-law! Wait till you see him! He must be the most handsome, the most intelligent boy in the whole world. He hasn't said two words yet but already I'm under the spell and your daughter will be absolutely gob-smacked when she sees him.

ARGAN: (*To CLEANTE who is about to go.*) Oh don't go, sir. My daughter is getting married and they've brought her fiancé over to visit her. You see, she hasn't actually seen him yet.

CLEANTE: I am deeply honoured, sir, that you'd like me to witness this momentous meeting.

ARGAN: He's the son of a very successful doctor and they're going to be married in just four days time.

CLEANTE: Lovely.

ARGAN: Do tell her music teacher so that he can come to the wedding.

CLEANTE: I won't forget.

ARGAN: Oh, and I'd like you to come as well.

CLEANTE: I am greatly honoured.

TOINETTE: Come on now, stand to attention. Here they come.

M. DIAFOIRUS and THOMAS enter.

Scene 5

ARGAN: (*Putting his hand on his cap without taking it off.*) Forgive me, sir, but for medical reasons M. Purgon has forbidden me to uncover my head. You're in the same profession so I'm sure you'll understand why.

M. DIAFOIRUS: Don't concern yourself, sir, I beseech you. Wherever we go, we doctors try to bring only succour to the sick never anxiety.

ARGAN and M. DIAFOIRUS speak at the same time, interrupting and confusing each other.

ARGAN	M. DIAFOIRUS
Sir, I greet you with heartfelt joy.	Sir, we come here, my son Thomas and I,

You do me a great honour to let you know
and I only wish the overwhelming
happiness
that I had been able to come we feel at the favour
to your house you bestow on us
to assure you of the depth in wishing to receive us
of my feelings! into this affectionate
However no-one knows and respectful alliance
better than you sir with your family and you
the plight of poor sick people. can be certain that in all
All I can do is to medical matters and,
say to you here and now indeed, in all things,
that I will seek every we are, and shall be,
opportunity
to let you know that sir
I am and shall be, sir entirely at your service.
entirely at your service!

M. DIAFOIRUS: (*Turns to his son and says to him.*) Come along, Thomas. Step forward. Pay your respects.

THOMAS: (*A great big sheepish blockhead, fresh out of school, who does everything awkwardly.*) Should I begin with the father?

M. DIAFOIRUS: Yes.

THOMAS: (*To ARGON.*) Sir, I have come to salute, to acknowledge, to embrace and to venerate in you a second father and a second father to whom I owe more than to the first. The first sired me, but you chose me. Nature gave me to him but you were kind enough to pick me. I am obliged to him for the work of his body but I am obliged to you for the work of your imagination and since the power of the mind is greater than any corporal function so I owe you more and so I prize this proposed alliance. I have come here today to lay before you, in anticipation, my very humble and very respectful thanks.

TOINETTE: Well, thank God for schools and colleges. They turn out such very clever people.

THOMAS: How did I do, father?

M. DIAFOIRUS: Very well, Thomas, very well.

ARGAN: (*To ANGELIQUE.*) Come along, Angelique, welcome the young gentleman.

THOMAS: Do I have to kiss her?

M. DIAFOIRUS: Yes, of course you do.

THOMAS: (*Kisses ANGELIQUE on the cheek – not the hand – according to the custom of the period.*) Madam, heaven has rightly decided that it is proper for you to be called Mother-in-Law...

ARGAN: That's not my wife – that's my daughter!

THOMAS: Where is your wife?

ARGAN: She's coming.

THOMAS: Will I wait until she comes, father?

M. DIAFOIRUS: Pay your respects to the young lady, Thomas.

THOMAS: You may recall, mademoiselle, that the statue of Memnon, when hit by the rays of the sun, yielded a euphonious sound and in the same way I feel a thrill of passionate ecstasy on seeing your beauty which blazes like the sun. Botanists tell us that a flower called the Heliotrope always turns its face towards that glorious lamp of heaven, so will my heart forever turn towards those glorious lamps, your adorable eyes. From now until the end of time they will be my only focus. Allow me, mademoiselle, on this special day to place on the altar of your beauty the sacrifice of my heart – that heart which for the rest of its life will seek no other glory than to be your most humble, most obedient and most faithful servant and husband.

TOINETTE: (*In jest.*) Education is a great thing. You can learn to put things so nicely.

ARGAN: (*To CLEANTE.*) Well sir, what have you got to say to that? He's performing brilliantly. If he's as good a doctor as he is an orator it'll be a pleasure to be one of his patients.

TOINETTE: It certainly will. I'll be astonished if his cures are as good as his speeches.

ARGAN: Come along quickly, my chair and seats for everyone. You sit there Angelique. You see, sir, everyone likes your son and I must say you're a lucky man to be blessed with a child like that.

M. DIAFOIRUS: I know that I'm his father, sir, but I can say in all honesty that I have good reason to be pleased with him. Everyone who knows him says that he's incapable of being naughty. You see, he's never had an active imagination. He's never had the kind of fiery passion that one notices in some young people and it's because of this that I've always been optimistic about his sense of judgement. As a child he was never what one might call quick on the draw. In fact, he wasn't quick at anything. He has always been gentle, quiet and shy, never said a word, and never played silly childish games, thank God. We did have great difficulty in teaching him to read. Actually, he was nine years old before he knew the alphabet. "Excellent" I said to myself, "the tree which bears the late fruit bears the best fruit"; "it's easier to carve on sand than on marble but what is carved on marble remains", "his slowness and his slack imagination are signs of a good sense of judgement". When I sent him to college he found it very difficult but he strove against adversity and his tutors always praised him for his diligence and hard work. Finally by sticking at it through thick and thin I'm delighted to say he obtained his primary degree.

In the two years since then no graduate has made more
noise in the college debates. He is held in dread by
everyone and no matter what motion is proposed he
will argue against it to the bitter end. He is unyielding
in debate, rigid as a Turk. He never changes his mind
and follows his arguments to the last bastion of logic.
What pleases me most about him is that he follows my
example and without question accepts all traditional
opinions. He has absolutely no desire to understand or
even to listen to the ideas or experiments that led to the
so-called discoveries of this century, like the ridiculous
notion that blood circulates through the body and other
such nonsense.

THOMAS: (*Drawing out a huge very ornate illuminated roll
containing his thesis, and presenting it to ANGELIQUE.*)
I have written a thesis opposing the theory of blood
circulation and with your permission, sir, I would like to
present it to your daughter as the first fruit of my talent!

ANGELIQUE: I would have no use for it sir. I know
nothing about such things.

TOINETTE: Give it to me, give it to me. It's got some
lovely pictures on it. It'll look great on my bedroom wall.

THOMAS: With your father's permission, I would like to
invite you, one of these days to come and watch a woman
being dissected. I have to write a thesis on dissection.

TOINETTE: What fun! Now some men take their
girlfriends to see a play – but to go to a dissection –
that's really romantic.

M. DIAFOIRUS: It is now my duty to refer to those
specific attributes necessary for marriage and
propagation. I can assure you Thomas has been
examined by our own doctors and would seem to have
all the necessary equipment. He has an absolutely

huge... libido and I believe that he has the right kind of temperament to fertilise and beget healthy children.

ARGAN: Do you intend, sir, to present him at court and get him a post as a court physician?

M. DIAFOIRUS: To be completely honest, sir, it's never a good idea for a doctor to treat important people. I prefer to work with the general public. The public are obliging. A doctor is never responsible for his actions with the general public and as long as he sticks to the basic rules he doesn't have to worry about what happens to them. On the other hand, when important people get sick they insist that their doctors make them better.

TOINETTE: How inconsiderate! You can't be expected to cure them; you only make out prescriptions and collect your fees – they ought to be able to cure themselves.

M. DIAFOIRUS: That's absolutely true. They expect far too much of us.

ARGAN: (*To CLEANTE.*) Sir, do you think you could persuade my daughter to sing a little something for us?

CLEANTE: I was hoping you might ask. I thought you might be amused if your daughter and I sang a scene from a little operatic work that's only just been written. (*To ANGELIQUE.*) Here's your part.

ANGELIQUE: My part?

CLEANTE: (*To ANGELIQUE.*) Please don't refuse. Just let me describe what happens in the scene. (*To everyone.*) I must confess that I can't sing very well but I might be able to make myself understood and I know you'll all make allowances because my main purpose is to support Mademoiselle Angelique.

ARGAN: Is it a good story?

CLEANTE: It's really a kind of improvised piece. The libretto's in a sort of rhythmical prose very similar to free verse. The overall effect is to give the illusion of two people trying to express their passion in spontaneous song, singing the first words that come into their heads.

ARGAN: It sounds very interesting. We'll listen to it.

CLEANTE takes on the character of a shepherd and explains to his mistress how he has loved her since their last meeting and then they reveal their thoughts to each other by singing.

CLEANTE: This is the background to the scene. Once upon a time there was a shepherd who went to the theatre to see a play. He got completely wrapped up in the glamour of the performance, when, not long after it had begun, he was distracted by a noise coming from behind him. He had turned around and saw a big bully insulting a shepherdess with rude words. Immediately he leapt to the defence of the fair sex, to whom every man owes duty. After seeing off the bully he approached the shepherdess and beheld a young woman with the most wonderful eyes. Tears trickled gently from those eyes but they were the most exquisite tears he had ever seen. "God in heaven", he thought to himself. "How could anyone ever insult such a lovely creature. Could any living soul, even a barbarian, not be moved by those tears." He lifted his hand and gently wiped away the tears which he had found so appealing. The tender-hearted shepherdess thanked him for this trivial service in such a charming, tender and passionate way that the shepherd was completely captivated. Each word, each look, was like a fiery arrow piercing his heart. "What act on earth" he said to himself, "can deserve such delicate words of thanks. What would a man not do, what service would he not render, what danger would he not brave, willingly, to attract, for even one moment, the nectarous delightfulness of this most appreciative

soul?" Meanwhile the play continued and he didn't
even notice but the curtain fell too quickly because
when the applause died down he realised that he
would have to leave this seraphic shepherdess. He
carried home with him the memory of that first
glimpse. A love was born as intense as any love that
might have flourished over many years. Before long
he was whipped by the lash of absence, flailed by the
scourge of no longer seeing her whom he had glanced
at so fleetingly. He did everything in his power to see
her again. He was haunted night and day, day and
night by that beatific vision – but all in vain. The
shepherdess was kept under lock and key and guarded
so strictly that it was impossible to get near her. The
raging thirst in his heart had now become insatiable
and in the violence of his passion he decided to plead
for this divine angel's hand in marriage. He asked her
permission to do this by means of a note which he
cleverly arranged to be delivered into her fair hands.
He knew that without her, life would not be worth
living. However, at the same time, he hears that her
father has arranged for her to marry someone else. He
is told that preparations are in full swing for a wedding
ceremony. Try to imagine, if you will, what a cruel
blow this is to the heart of our sad shepherd. Look at
him! Look at him! Strapped on the wrack of desperate
despair. Picture him! Picture him! Crucified by
slaughtering sorrow. He cannot bear the disgusting
thought that he might see the creature he loves rapt in
the arms of another. But his constant love, love in
despair, love in desperation finds a way to let him
enter her home to find out how she is feeling and to
hear from her lips what fate might have in store for
him. He has barely entered her home when all is
revealed! He witnesses the arrival of that preposterous
suitor chosen at the whim of her father to stand in the
way of his righteous love. He sees his risible rival
standing beside his serene shepherdess like a comic

conqueror. The very sight of them fills him with feelings of frenzy that he can barely control. Common decency and the presence of her father prohibits the use of any language but the language of the eyes. He exchanges desolate glances with the creature that he loves. But at last, freeing himself from all restraints, the volcano of his passion erupts in song.

Sings.

> Fair Phyllis, fair Phyllis, I can suffer this no more
> Let us break, let us break our silence
> And to me your thoughts unfold
> I want to learn from you. I want to learn from you
> What fate may have in store
> Am I to live in joy and bliss, joy and bliss,
> Yes, joy and bliss
> Or in a grave lie cold, in a grave lie cold,
> In a grave lie cold?

ANGELIQUE (*Sings.*)

> Behold me Tircis, sad and forlorn
> Fear not, fear not
> Your Phyllis views these wedding plans with
> Contemptuous disdain, contemptuous, contemptuous,
> Contemptuous disdain
> I raise my eyes to God above and beg him
> To save me from my lot.
> I am in torment, I shake with fear,
> Please release me, please release me, release me
> From this bitter pain.

ARGAN: I had no idea that Angelique was so good at sightreading.

CLEANTE (*Sings.*)

> Fair Phyllis, fair Phyllis, oh how blessed would I be
> If you could find, if you could find within your bosom
> A special place for me

I want to hear you say, I want to hear you say
That we can be as one.

ANGELIQUE (*Sings.*)

I love you Tircis.

CLEANTE (*Sings.*)

What did you say?

ANGELIQUE (*Sings.*)

I love you.

CLEANTE (*Sings.*)

Say that once more.

ANGELIQUE (*Sings.*)

I love you, I love you, I love you.

CLEANTE (*Sings.*)

Oh lords of earth. Oh powers divine
No happiness is equal to mine
Just one more time oh let me hear
Those words that banish anguish and fear.

ANGELIQUE (*Sings.*)

I love you, I love you, I love you
I love you, I love you, I love you
I love you, I love you, I love you.

CLEANTE (*Sings.*)

Oh gentle Phyllis, do we forget
My rival, my rival.

ANGELIQUE (*Sings.*)

Your Phyllis hates the sight of him
She will never be his bride, never be his bride.
She'll never be his bride.

CLEANTE (*Sings.*)

Oh lovely Phyllis, we still forget
Your father, your father.

ANGELIQUE (*Sings.*)

Your Phyllis now would rather die
Than her father to obey.
Yes, she would rather die.
Yes, she would rather die
Than ever to obey.

CLEANTE (*Sings.*)

Come tempting death,
come take my soul

ANGELIQUE and CLEANTE (*Singing together.*)

For I'd rather die than let her/him go
Your/my cruel father do/I'll not obey
Please/I'll ignore him, disregard him
Your/my father you/I will not obey.

ARGAN: And what does the father have to say to all this?

CLEANTE: Nothing.

ARGAN: He must be a really stupid kind of father to put
up with all that nonsense and still say nothing.

CLEANTE (*Starting to sing.*)

Fair Phyllis, fair Phyllis.

ARGAN: Thank you! Thank you! I think we've heard
enough of that. Your play is setting a very bad
example. This shepherd Tircis, is an arrogant lout and
as for that shepherdess, Phyllis, she's a shameless
hussy to speak like that in front of her father. Let me
see the score. Wait a minute! What are the words
you've been singing? There's only a bit of music
written here.

CLEANTE: Didn't you know, sir, they've discovered a new way of writing the music and the words in the notes?

ARGAN: Have they indeed? Goodbye sir, thank you for everything, but we could have done without your idiotic opera.

CLEANTE: I was only trying to entertain you.

CLEANTE exits.

ARGAN: That kind of rubbish is never entertaining. Ah, here comes my wife.

BELINE enters.

Scene 6

ARGAN: My darling, come and meet M. Diafoirus and his son, Thomas.

THOMAS: (*Begins reciting a speech that he has prepared earlier but his memory fails him and he can't continue.*) Madam, heaven has rightly decided that it is proper for you to be called Mother-in-Law, for in your face we see...

BELINE: Sir, I'm so glad that I got here in time to have the honour of making your acquaintance.

THOMAS: For in your face we see... For in your face we see... Look, you've interrupted me in the middle of my sentence and now I can't remember what I was going to say.

M. DIAFOIRUS: Thomas, save it for another time.

ARGAN: Oh Mimsy, I wish you had been here earlier.

TOINETTE: Yes, madam, if only you'd been here you'd have heard all about the second father, the statue of Memnon and the flower called Heliotrope.

ARGAN: Now, come along Angelique, join hands with Thomas and promise to be his bride.

ANGELIQUE: Daddy!

ARGAN: What do you mean "Daddy"!

ANGELIQUE: Please, please don't rush things. Just give us time to get to know each other, to see if we're attracted to each other. Attraction is important if we're to have a satisfying marriage.

THOMAS: As far as I'm concerned, Angelique, I'm already attracted to you. I don't need to wait any longer.

ANGELIQUE: I don't care how attracted you are to me. I'm not attracted to you. In fact, I have to say that nothing about you has made any impression on me at all.

ARGAN: Take it easy. There'll be enough time for all that sort of thing after you're married.

ANGELIQUE: Please, father, please give me time. Marriage is a leash which no heart should be forced to wear, and, if this gentleman is at all honourable he won't want to accept a woman who is given to him in a straightjacket.

THOMAS: Faulty logic, Angelique, faulty logic. Being a man of honour does not preclude taking you from your father.

ANGELIQUE: It is morally wrong to try to make someone love you by force.

THOMAS: When we read about our ancestors, Angelique, we learn that it was their custom to kidnap their brides-to-be from their fathers' houses by force so that no woman would ever seem to fall into a man's arms willingly.

ANGELIQUE: Our ancestors, sir, are our ancestors; the past is the past but we are living in the present and that kind of grotesque display isn't necessary nowadays. When a marriage is right you know that it's right and no-one has to be forced into it. Have patience. If you really love me sir, you would want what I want.

THOMAS: I would, but not when it gets in the way of my passions.

ANGELIQUE: The greatest sign of love is to be able to yield to the wishes of the person you love.

THOMAS: Allow me, mademoiselle, to refine a distinction: in matters which do not involve the ownership of the woman by the man I concede, but in matters which directly concern the male's ownership of his partner I must object.

TOINETTE: What an orator! The young gentleman is straight out of university, Angelique, he's bound to win every time. Why do you keep resisting him? How can you refuse the honour of being accepted into the groves of Academe?

BELINE: Perhaps she's got her eye on someone else.

ANGELIQUE: And if I had madam I assure you that my choice would be a true and honest choice.

ARGAN: Dear me, all of this is making me look like a right idiot.

BELINE: If I were you, Bubba, I wouldn't force her to get married. Oh no! I know exactly what I would do!

ANGELIQUE: I know what you're trying to say madam. I know what you'd like to do. Well, you won't get what you want.

BELINE: If I don't, it'll be because very clever and very polite daughters like you, make fun of their fathers' wishes. It wasn't like that in my day.

ANGELIQUE: A daughter's duty has limits, madam.

BELINE: That's as much as to say you've got your heart set on marriage and want to pick a husband to gratify your own desires.

ANGELIQUE: If my father won't let me have a husband who satisfies me I would beseech him, at least, not to force me to marry someone whom I cannot love.

ARGAN: Gentlemen, I'm really sorry about all this.

ANGELIQUE: Everyone has their own reason for getting married. Since I myself want a husband whom I can love and with whom I intend to live for the rest of my life, I confess that I will take great care in trying to find one. Some get married just to get away from their parents, some to be able to do what they please and some people, madam, see marriage as a purely commercial proposition. Some women get married only to make money. There are even some who can't wait for their husbands to die so they can benefit from their wills. They run, without shame, from husband to husband pocketing their booty. Such women, to speak the truth, don't care about human emotions and have little or no self-respect.

BELINE: I find you extremely quarrelsome today and I would very much like to know exactly what you meant by all that.

ANGELIQUE: Me, madam? I meant exactly what I said.

BELINE: Sweetheart, you've become so stupid one no longer knows how to begin to tolerate you.

ANGELIQUE: You'd really love to force me, madam, to answer you back impolitely but I warn you that I won't give you that pleasure.

BELINE: Your rudeness is insufferable.

ANGELIQUE: Go on, madam, say whatever you like.

BELINE: Your ridiculous pride and your foolish vanity make you feel superior to everyone else.

ANGELIQUE: It's no use, madam. I'll be well-behaved in spite of you and in order to remove all hope of your success I will remove myself from your sight.

ARGAN: Listen to me. There's no middle ground in all of this. You choose. In four days time you marry this young gentleman or else you go into a convent.

ANGELIQUE exits.

(*To BELINE.*) Don't upset yourself. I'll deal with her.

BELINE: I'm really sorry, darling, but I have to leave you. I've got something to do in town which I can't put off. I'll be back soon.

ARGAN: You go, my love and don't forget to call in at the notary's office to see how he's getting on with that little bit of business.

BELINE: Bye, bye Bubba.

ARGAN: Bye, bye Mimsy.

BELINE exits.

That woman really loves me. It's unbelievable.

M. DIAFOIRUS: We must, sir, take our leave of you.

ARGAN: I beg you, sir, to tell me briefly how I am.

M. DIAFOIRUS: (*Taking his pulse.*) Come along, Thomas, take the gentleman's other arm. Feel his pulse and let's see if you can diagnose it properly. What have you got to say?

THOMAS: I would say... this gentleman's pulse is the pulse of a man who is... not well.

M. DIAFOIRUS: Good.

THOMAS: That it is a modicum slow; one might even say... very slow.

M. DIAFOIRUS: Good.

THOMAS: Forceful.

M. DIAFOIRUS: Yes.

THOMAS: And even a little irregular.

M. DIAFOIRUS: Excellent.

THOMAS: This indicates an imbalance in the splenetic parenchyma; that's to say, the spleen.

ARGAN: Oh no! M. Purgon says it's my liver that's poorly.

M. DIAFOIRUS: Yes indeed. When one talks about the parenchyma one refers to both the liver and the spleen because of the strong connection between them by means of the lower intestine, the pylorus and often the gastrointestinal tract. Undoubtedly he has ordered you to eat a great deal of roast beef.

ARGAN: No, nothing but boiled beef.

M. DIAFOIRUS: Yes, indeed. Roast beef, boiled beef – same thing. He's given you excellent advice. You couldn't be in better hands.

ARGAN: Sir, would you please tell me how many grains of salt I should put on an egg?

M. DIAFOIRUS: Six, eight, ten – as long as it's an even number. The same with pills – always take an odd number.

ARGAN: Thank you sir – until we meet again. Goodbye sir.

M. DIAFOIRUS and THOMAS exeunt. BELINE enters.

Scene 7

BELINE: I've just popped in, my love, before going out to tell you something that I thought you ought to know.

I was passing Angelique's bedroom and there was a young man in there with her who ran away when he saw me.

ARGAN: A young man with my daughter, in her bedroom?

BELINE: Yes. Your younger daughter, Louison, was with them. She'll be able to tell you all about it.

ARGAN: Send her here, my love, send her here.

BELINE exits.

Oh the shameless slut. Now I'm beginning to understand her stubbornness.

LOUISON enters.

Scene 8

LOUISON: What is it Daddy? My step-mother said you wanted to see me.

ARGAN: Yes, I do. Come here. Forward. Turn around. Look up. Look at me. Well?

LOUISON: What Daddy?

ARGAN: Now then?

LOUISON: What?

ARGAN: Have you nothing to tell me?

LOUISON: If you're bored I could tell you the story of *The Ass's Skin* or if you prefer I could tell you the fable of *The Crow and the Fox.* I learned them recently.

ARGAN: That's not what I'm asking you about.

LOUISON: What is it then?

ARGAN: Oh clever clogs, you know perfectly well what I'm talking about.

LOUISON: I beg your pardon Daddy.

ARGAN: Is this how you obey me?

LOUISON: What do you mean?

ARGAN: Haven't I told you to come and tell me, straight away, everything, you see?

LOUISON: Yes, Daddy.

ARGAN: Have you done that?

LOUISON: Yes, Daddy.

ARGAN: Haven't you seen anything today?

LOUISON: No, Daddy.

ARGAN: No?

LOUISON: No, Daddy.

ARGAN: You're sure?

LOUISON: I'm sure.

ARGAN: Is that so? Well, I'll just have to make you see something then, won't I? (*He gets a handful of birches.*)

LOUISON: Oh, Daddy.

ARGAN: You wicked little toad. You didn't tell me you'd seen a man in your sister's bedroom, did you?

LOUISON: Daddy!

ARGAN: I'll teach you not to lie.

LOUISON: (*Throwing herself on her knees.*) Oh Daddy. I'm really, really sorry. Please forgive me. My sister told me not to tell you but I will, I will, I'll tell you everything.

ARGAN: First you've got to be beaten for telling lies.

LOUISON: Please forgive me Daddy.

ARGAN: No.

LOUISON: Dearest Daddy, please don't beat me.

ARGAN: You must be beaten.

LOUISON: In the name of God, Daddy, don't beat me.

ARGAN: (*Grabbing her to beat her.*) Come here. Come here.

LOUISON: Oh Daddy, you're really hurting me. Stop! Stop! Oh I'm dead – I'm dead. (*She pretends to be dead.*)

ARGAN: Oh no! What's happened? Louison! Louison! Oh my God! My daughter! Oh poor me! My dearest daughter is dead. What have I done? Damn those bitches! A plague on these birches! Oh my child, my daughter, my poor little Louison.

LOUISON: There, there, Daddy. Don't cry. I'm not completely dead.

ARGAN: You little trickster. Oh well! I'll forgive you just this once, on condition that you really tell me everything.

LOUISON: I will, Daddy.

ARGAN: Be very careful because here is a little finger which knows everything and this little finger will tell me if you are lying.

LOUISON: Daddy, please don't tell my sister that I've told you.

ARGAN: I won't.

LOUISON: Well, Daddy, a man came into my sister's bedroom while I was there.

ARGAN: And then?

LOUISON: I asked him what he wanted and he told me that he was her singing teacher.

ARGAN: I see, I see. So that's his game. And then?

LOUISON: And then my sister came in.

ARGAN: And then?

LOUISON: She said to him "Go away! Go away. My God, go away! You will drive me to desperation!"

ARGAN: And then?

LOUISON: He didn't want to go.

ARGAN: What did he say to her?

LOUISON: He said all kinds of things to her.

ARGAN: Yes?

LOUISON: He said a bit of this and a bit of that. He said he loved her a lot and that she was the most beautiful girl in the whole world.

ARGAN: And after that?

LOUISON: After that he went down on his knees before her.

ARGAN: And after that?

LOUISON: After that he kissed her hands.

ARGAN: And after that?

LOUISON: After that, my stepmother came to the door and he ran away.

ARGAN: Is there nothing else?

LOUISON: No Daddy.

ARGAN: My little finger is muttering something. (*He puts his finger to his ear.*) Listen. I see! I see! Oh yes, oh yes, I see: my little finger says you saw something else and you're not telling me what it is.

LOUISON: Oh Daddy, your little finger's a liar.

ARGAN: Be careful.

LOUISON: No, Daddy. I promise you your little finger is telling lies. Don't believe it.

ARGAN: All right, all right, we'll see. Off you go now and take good care of yourself. Go.

LOUISON exits.

What's the matter with children today? What a mess. I haven't even got enough time to think about my illness. Honest to God, I can't go on much longer.

BERALDE enters.

Scene 9

BERALDE: What's wrong brother? How are you?

ARGAN: Oh Beralde, my dear brother. I'm very sick.

BERALDE: What do you mean, "very sick"?

ARGAN: I am in a dreadful decline.

BERALDE: That's terrible.

ARGAN: I've hardly got the strength to speak.

BERALDE: I've come here for a reason, brother. I'd like to suggest a husband for Angelique.

ARGAN: (*Speaking angrily and getting up from his chair.*) Don't talk to me about that whore. She's a cheat, a trollop, a hussy and I'm going to put her into a convent in two days time.

BERALDE: That's fine. I'm glad you're getting your strength back. My visits are obviously doing you good. We'll talk later. I've brought along an entertainment for you. It'll get rid of your depression and put you in a much better frame of mind for what we have to talk about. I've brought along one of the actresses, performing in the Carnival, to sing a song for you here in your room. You'll love it. It will do you as much good as one of M. Purgon's cures. Listen to her. Toinette, please show in the young lady. Come in Mademoiselle. Allow me to introduce my brother.

TOINETTE brings in the ACTRESS.

ARGAN: Forgive me mademoiselle, I'm a very sick man.

ACTRESS: I am at your service sir.

BERALDE: Give me your music, mademoiselle, and I'll attempt to accompany you on this old instrument, if it still works.

BERALDE sits at the harmonium to accompany her.

ACTRESS: I would be delighted.

Sings.

> Springtime will not last forever
> Winter takes its place
> Youth is but a passing treasure
> Time will soon efface.
> So
> Love while you can
> Don't waste one precious moment
> Love while you can.
> Just relish the excitement
> Old age comes too fast
> Beauty will not last
> So love, now
> Love while you can.
> The price of joy is pain and heartache
> Lovers come and go
> Delight at night then grief at daybreak

Yes, it's often so.
Still
Love while you can
Don't waste one precious moment.
Love while you can.
Just relish the excitement
Old age comes too fast
Beauty will not last
So love, love
Love while you can.
Are the pleasures worth the payments
Should we never start?
With each woe, such sweet endearments
Captivate your heart
That you must
Love while you can
Don't waste one precious moment
Love while you can.
Just relish the excitement
Old age comes too fast
Beauty will not last
So love, now
Love while you can.

BERALDE, TOINETTE and ARGAN applaud.

BERALDE: That was very beautiful. Thank you
    mademoiselle. Toinette, show the young lady out.

*TOINETTE opens the door for the door for the ACTRESS who
exits.*

ACT THREE

Scene 1

BERALDE: Well, brother, what d'you think of that? Much better for you than a dose of sennapods, isn't it?

TOINETTE: Now listen, there's nothing wrong with a good dose of sennapods.

BERALDE: D'you think you're ready to have our little chat together?

ARGAN: (*Going off, presumably to the toilet.*) In a minute, brother, be patient. I'll be back.

TOINETTE: Wait sir, wait. Don't forget you can't walk without your stick.

ARGAN: You're right, of course. You're right.

Scene 2

TOINETTE: Please don't desert your niece in her hour of need.

BERALDE: Don't worry, I'll do everything I can to get her what she wants.

TOINETTE: We've got to put an end once and for all to this ridiculous marriage that he's dreamed up for her. Wouldn't it be a good idea if we could pay a doctor to come here, and say whatever we wanted him to say? We could get him to attack M. Purgon's reputation and turn the master against him. I know we haven't got anyone on hand to do this for us but I've decided to try something off the top of my head.

BERALDE: What?

TOINETTE: Well, it's a ludicrous idea. It probably won't work but it might just be fun. Leave it to me. You keep playing your part and when he comes back I'll do what I have to do. God help me. (*Loud farting noises from ARGAN's rooms.*) God help us all.

She exits.

Scene 3

ARGAN: I'm glad you're still here Beralde. Please help me into my chair. Now listen, I'm exhausted.

BERALDE: I hope you don't mind, brother, but first and foremost I've got to ask you not to lose your temper while we're talking.

ARGAN: Of course I won't.

BERALDE: To react calmly to everything I have to say to you.

ARGAN: Yes.

BERALDE: And to think logically and dispassionately about what we have to discuss.

ARGAN: Good God, yes! What a formal preface.

BERALDE: How is it, brother, when you have so much wealth, when you have no children except the one daughter, because I don't count that little one – I put it to you – how is it you are talking of putting her into a convent?

ARGAN: How is it, brother, when I am master in my own house you suggest that I can't do whatever I like?

BERALDE: Is it your wife who has advised you to jettison your two daughters like this? Oh, I'm sure that in her own loving way she'd be overjoyed to see them both become model nuns.

ARGAN: Ah, I see, now we have it! The first thing you do is to drag that poor woman into it. Everyone wants to believe that in some way she's the root of all evil.

BERALDE: Oh no, brother, don't say that! She's a woman who wants the best for your family, who never thinks about herself, who is absolutely devoted to you and who shows an incredible amount of affection and kindness towards your children – that's certain! Don't let's talk about her. Let's get back to your daughter. What's the big idea behind wanting to marry her to a doctor's son?

ARGAN: My idea, brother, is to provide myself with a useful son-in-law.

BERALDE: That's not what your daughter wants, brother, and someone else has turned up who would suit her much better.

ARGAN: Yes, brother, but the first one would suit me much better.

BERALDE: But is she going to choose a husband, brother, for herself or for you?

ARGAN: She must choose for herself, brother, and for me. I want to bring people into my family who are useful to me.

BERALDE: In that case, when your younger daughter grows up will you marry her off to an apothecary?

ARGAN: Why not?

BERALDE: Is it really possible you're always going to be putty in the hands of your apothecaries and your doctors? Are you always going to want to be sick in spite of everyone and everything?

ARGAN: What are you trying to say, brother?

BERALDE: I'm saying brother, that I've never laid eyes on a man who was less sick than you. No-one could ask for a better constitution than yours. The absolute proof that you're well and you've got a perfectly sound body is that, despite all your endeavour, you still haven't succeeded in damaging your health. You're still alive. None of the cures you've taken have managed to kill you.

ARGAN: You don't understand brother. Those medicaments keep me alive. M. Purgon says that I would die if three days went by without my receiving his care and attention.

BERALDE: If you don't watch out all his care and attention will guide you straight into the next world.

ARGAN: Let's take this a bit further, brother. So, you don't believe in medicine?

BERALDE: No, brother. I just don't believe that it's necessary for my welfare.

ARGAN: What! You mean, you don't believe in something that's accepted by everyone, something that's been respected for centuries?

BERALDE: Far from believing in it, I consider it, between ourselves, to be one of man's greatest follies. From a philosophical point of view, I can't imagine a more ludicrous farce. There's nothing quite so ridiculous as the sight of one man presuming that he can cure another man.

ARGAN: Why don't you want to admit, brother, that one man can cure another man?

BERALDE: Because, brother, the workings of our anatomies are mysteries. Mysteries which, up to the present, men don't see at all. Nature has put such a thick veil over our eyes that we can know nothing.

ARGAN: According to you, doctors know nothing?

BERALDE: That's right, brother. Oh, they know a lot about the classics, they speak good Latin, they can tell you the Greek names for all the illnesses, they can describe them and classify them but when it comes to curing them they know nothing at all.

ARGAN: All the same, you've got to admit that doctors know more about these things than other people.

BERALDE: They know what I've told you, brother, and that cures nothing. The virtue of their art is made up of bombastic balderdash and plausible prattle which gives you words instead of reasons and promises instead of results.

ARGAN: Nevertheless, brother, there are people in the world as wise and as clever as you and it's obvious that in times of sickness everyone needs a doctor.

BERALDE: That's a proof of human weakness not a confirmation of the reliability of medicine.

ARGAN: But doctors must believe in their skill because they make use of it for themselves.

BERALDE: That's because some of them do indeed believe in the popular illusion from which they make their money. There are others who don't believe in it but still make money. Your M. Purgon, for example, he's a real doctor. He's a medical man from head to toe. A man who believes in rules rather than mathematical proofs; who would think it a crime to want to question his rules; who sees nothing mysterious in medicine, nothing ambiguous, nothing difficult and who with the blindness of arrogance, the swiftness of confidence and with a subhuman grasp of common sense flings around prescriptions for enemas and bleedings never thinking about what he is doing. There's no point in bearing him ill-will for what he might do to you. He will kill you all in good faith doing no more to you than he does to his wife, his children and that he would do to himself, if necessary.

ARGAN: Oh brother, you've always had a grudge against him. Let's be realistic. What should a person do when he gets sick?

BERALDE: Nothing, brother.

ARGAN: Nothing?

BERALDE: Nothing. All that's needed is rest. Nature herself, if we let her, will gradually pull herself out of the disorder that she's fallen into. It's only our own fear and impatience that makes everything worse and most men die of their remedies not their diseases.

ARGAN: But you have to admit, brother, there must be ways in which we can help nature?

BERALDE: My God, brother, that's the sort of simplistic idea we love to indulge in, the sort of idea that men with good minds slip into accepting and we readily believe in because it flatters us and because we would like it to be true. When a doctor talks to you about helping, assisting and supporting nature; when he talks about reviving her and restoring her to full working order; when he tells you about purifying the blood, about refreshing the innards and the brain, about clearing the spleen, about improving the lungs, about curing the liver, about strengthening the heart, about restoring and maintaining correct body temperature and about holding the secrets of longer life, he's only telling you a fictional tale of medical romance. In the light of truth and experience you'll find there's nothing there at all. It's like waking up from a beautiful dream with no feeling except regret that it's not real.

ARGAN: That's like saying that all the world's knowledge is contained in your head. You seem to think you know more than all the great doctors of our day.

BERALDE: Your great doctors can seem like two different kinds of people depending on whether they're speaking or doing. Listen to them talk and they're the most brilliant people in the world; watch them at work and they're the stupidest of men.

ARGAN: Dear me, I can see you've suddenly become a great authority on the subject. I just wish there was a real doctor here to refute your arguments and take you down a peg or two.

BERALDE: Me, brother? I'm not in the business of waging war against the medical profession. Everyone, at their own risk, can think whatever they like. What I've said is only between ourselves. I'd like to have shown you something of the error of your ways and given you a laugh by taking you to see a play on this very subject by Molière.

ARGAN: This Molière of yours is a real smart Alec. Him and his plays. I think it's a scandal that he makes fun of decent people like doctors.

BERALDE: He isn't making fun of doctors. He's ridiculing the medical profession.

ARGAN: The man's an idiot. He's a presumptuous upstart to mock medical advice and medical prescriptions, to take it upon himself to challenge the entire medical profession and then to put respectable people, like doctors, on the stage.

BERALDE: What else should he put in his plays? He only writes about the different jobs that people do. You can see kings and princes on the stage every day and their backgrounds are every bit as respectable as any doctor's.

ARGAN: In the name of... everything evil, if I were a doctor I would love to get revenge on him for his arrogance. When he was very, very ill, I would leave him to die without any help or assistance. He could do what he liked and say what he liked but I wouldn't prescribe him even the smallest little bleeding or the smallest little enema. I'd say to him "die, die, die, you bastard, that'll teach you what it means to make fun of the medical profession".

BERALDE: You're very angry with him, aren't you?

ARGAN: Yes, I am. He's an ill-informed numbskull and if the doctors had any sense at all, they would do exactly what I say.

BERALDE: He'll have more sense than your doctors because he won't ask for their help.

ARGAN: Let him burn in the fires of hell, if he won't ask for medical help.

BERALDE: He has his reasons. He believes that only strong and healthy people have enough stamina to survive the remedies as well as the sickness. He knows he's only got enough stamina to survive the sickness.

ARGAN: What a stupid argument! Stop, brother, don't let's talk about this man any more. That kind of talk inflames my bile. You're making me sick.

BERALDE: All right, brother, we'll change the subject. Let's talk about your daughter. I don't think you ought to resort to locking her up in a convent because she's shown a little spirit. It's so extreme. Don't let your anger lead you blindly into picking the wrong son-in-law. Think of what your daughter wants. Remember that her marriage is going to affect the rest of her life.

M. FLEURANT comes in with his enema equipment.

Scene 4

ARGAN: Oh, please excuse me brother!

BERALDE: Why? What are you going to do?

ARGAN: I'm just going to have a little enema, it won't take long.

BERALDE: You must be joking. Can't you survive for one moment without colonic irrigation, without medicaments? Put it off till later. Relax for a little while.

ARGAN: M. Fleurant – come back this evening or tomorrow morning.

M. FLEURANT: Why are you interfering and contradicting medical advice? Why are you preventing M. Argan from taking my enema? You must be a very clever joker indeed to have such hubris.

BERALDE: Get out sir. It's easy to see you're not used to talking to people's faces.

M. FLEURANT: You shouldn't make fun of remedies in this way. You're wasting my time. I came here to administer a prescription. I'm going to tell M. Purgon how I've been prevented from carrying out his orders and from performing my duty. You'll see... you'll see...

ARGAN: Oh brother, you'll be the cause of some terrible catastrophe.

BERALDE: The terrible catastrophe of missing an enema, prescribed by M. Purgon. Is there no way to cure you of this affliction, this obsession with doctors? Are you going to spend the rest of your life drowning in their remedies?

ARGAN: My God, brother, you're only talking like this because you're fit and well. If you were in my shoes you'd soon change your tune. It's easy to speak out against medicine when you're in good health.

BERALDE: What exactly is wrong with you?

ARGAN: You'll drive me mad. I really wish you had my illness to see if you'd still talk this kind of nonsense. Ah! Here is M. Purgon.

M. PURGON comes in with TOINETTE.

Scene 5

M. PURGON: I've just heard an interesting piece of news down there at the door. I've just heard that someone, here in this house is making fun of my prescriptions and that the remedies which I have prescribed are being refused.

ARGAN: Sir, it's not...

M. PURGON: This looks like a case of extreme hubris; an extraordinary kind of revolution: the patient rebelling against his doctor.

TOINETTE: That's shocking!

M. PURGON: An enema that I had taken great pleasure in making up myself...

ARGAN: It's not me.

M. PURGON: Conceived and prepared according to all the rules of my profession...

TOINETTE: It's wrong!

M. PURGON: Which would have had a miraculous effect on your bowels.

ARGAN: It's my brother...

M. PURGON: To superciliously send it back...

ARGAN: It's him...

M. PURGON: It's a monstrous outrage.

TOINETTE: It certainly is.

M. PURGON: A truly indecent assault on medicine...

ARGAN: It's all his fault...

M. PURGON: An act of high treason perpetrated against the entire medical profession for which no punishment would be too severe.

TOINETTE: You're absolutely right.

M. PURGON: I am bound to tell you that from this moment you are no longer my patient...

ARGAN: It's my brother...

M. PURGON: That I do not wish to have anything whatsoever to do with you...

TOINETTE: You won't regret it!

M. PURGON: To completely terminate all connection with you, here is the deed of gift I made for my nephew as a wedding present!

He violently rips up the deed of gift.

ARGAN: It's my brother who's made a mess of everything!

M. PURGON: To make fun of my enema!

ARGAN: Bring it here! I'll have it now!

M. PURGON: I was so close to curing you of all your ailments.

TOINETTE: He doesn't deserve to be cured!

M. PURGON: I was going to clean out your entire system and get rid of everything nasty.

ARGAN: Brother!

M. PURGON: I'd have needed to give you only a dozen more treatments to flush out the whole mess.

TOINETTE: He's not worth the trouble.

M. PURGON: However, since you don't wish to be cured by my hands...

ARGAN: It's not my fault!

M. PURGON: Since you disregard the obedience owed to a doctor...

TOINETTE: That cries out for vengeance!

M. PURGON: Since you have declared yourself an insurrectionist against the cures that I've prescribed for you...

ARGAN: Oh no! Not at all!

M. PURGON: I'm bound to tell you that I'm leaving you alone with your failing constitution, with your weak bowels, with your poisoned blood, with your acidic bile and with your fetid humours...

TOINETTE: That's the best possible thing you could do!

ARGAN: My God!

M. PURGON: I predict that within four days your condition will be incurable...

ARGAN: Please, M. Purgon, have mercy on me!

M. PURGON: That you will fall into bradypepsia...

ARGAN: M. Purgon!

M. PURGON: From bradypepsia into dyspepsia...

ARGAN: M. Purgon!

M. PURGON: From dyspepsia into apepsia...

ARGAN: M. Purgon!

M. PURGON: From apepsia into diarrhoea...

ARGAN: M. Purgon!

M. PURGON: From diarrhoea into dysentery...

ARGAN: M. Purgon!

M. PURGON: From dysentery into dropsy...

ARGAN: M. Purgon!

M. PURGON: From dropsy into loss of life – all brought down upon you by your own foolishness.

M. PURGON exits with TOINETTE.

Scene 6

ARGAN: Oh my God, I'm a dead man. Brother, you've destroyed me.

BERALDE: How? What's wrong?

ARGAN: I'm completely ruined. Medicine's taking its revenge. I can feel it.

BERALDE: Honestly, brother, you're mad. I wouldn't like people to see you carrying on like this. Please think clearly for a minute. Pull yourself together and don't let your imagination run away with you.

ARGAN: You heard it for yourself, brother. You heard the weird diseases that he's threatened me with.

BERALDE: You're so gullible!

ARGAN: He said that within four days my condition would be incurable.

BERALDE: Does that mean that it's going to happen? Is he some kind of soothsayer? To listen to you, anyone would think that M. Purgon held your life line in the palm of his own hand and that by some supreme authority he could lengthen it or shorten it as he pleased. You've got to realise that your life is your own! The chances of your being killed by M. Purgon's anger are as slight as the chances of your being kept alive by his remedies. Here's a real opportunity, if you want it, to rid yourself of doctors for ever, or, if you absolutely can't live without them, it's easy to find another one, brother, with whom you may run a little less risk.

ARGAN: Oh brother, if only you understood the complexities of my physical make-up, if only you knew how I have to take care of myself.

BERALDE: What I really do know, what I really do understand is that you're a very blinkered man with a most peculiar view of life indeed.

TOINETTE comes in.

Scene 7

TOINETTE: Sir, a doctor has called to see you.

ARGAN: What doctor?

TOINETTE: A doctor of medicine.

ARGAN: Who is he?

TOINETTE: I don't know him but he and I are as alike as two peas in a pod and if I wasn't certain that my mother was a respectable woman I'd think he was my little brother, born after my father's death.

ARGAN: Bring him in.

She exits.

BERALDE: Well, you've got what you wanted. One doctor leaves, another arrives.

ARGAN: I'm terrified you're going to cause trouble.

BERALDE: You're always saying that.

ARGAN: I'm very worried about all these diseases that I don't know about... these...

TOINETTE comes in dressed as a doctor.

Scene 8

TOINETTE: I hope you don't mind my visiting you and that you'll allow me to humbly offer you my services for any blood lettings and colonic irrigations you might require.

ARGAN: I'm greatly obliged to you, sir. Good heavens, that's Toinette.

TOINETTE: Please excuse me, sir, I've forgotten to give a message to my servant. I'll be back in a minute.

She exits.

ARGAN: Don't you think that's really Toinette?

BERALDE: Well... there is certainly an extraordinary resemblance but it's not the first time that such things have been seen. There are many stories based on such tricks of nature.

ARGAN: I'm amazed. I don't know what to say.

TOINETTE comes back in. She has changed her costume so quickly that it's difficult to believe that it was she who appeared as the "Doctor".

Scene 9

TOINETTE: What do you want sir?

ARGAN: What?

TOINETTE: Didn't you call me?

ARGAN: No, I didn't.

TOINETTE: I must have been hearing things.

ARGAN: Stay for a minute and see how much the doctor looks like you.

TOINETTE: I told you that but I won't stay, thank you very much. I've got work to do below and anyway I've seen enough of him. (*She exits.*)

ARGAN: If I hadn't seen the two of them I would have absolutely believed they were the same person.

BERALDE: I've read astonishing things about resemblances of this kind and, recently, we've seen cases where everyone has been taken in.

ARGAN: I must say I would have been fooled by this one. I could have sworn they were the same person.

TOINETTE comes in, dressed as the "Doctor".

Scene 10

TOINETTE: I'm really sorry about that, sir.

ARGAN: It's amazing!

TOINETTE: Please forgive my curiosity in wanting to see a famous invalid like yourself. Your reputation, which is talked about everywhere, tempted me. You must excuse the liberty I've taken.

ARGAN: I'm at your service, sir.

TOINETTE: I notice, sir, that you're staring at me. What age do you think I am?

ARGAN: You can be no more than twenty-six or twenty-seven.

TOINETTE: Ah! Ahhh! Ahhhh! I'm ninety!

ARGAN: Ninety?

TOINETTE: Yes! You see, one of the results of my secret skills is to keep me well preserved, youthful and strong.

ARGAN: Upon my word, you're a fine-looking, juvenile old man of ninety.

TOINETTE: I am a travelling doctor who wanders from town to town, from province to province, from realm to realm searching for famous cases which might interest me, finding patients worthy of my attention and suitable for me to practice on them the great and wonderful medical discoveries that I've made. I refuse to trifle with any run of the mill rubbish. I won't concern myself with ordinary illnesses. I despise frivolities like rheumatisms, mild inflammations, slight fevers, hysterics and nervous headaches. I long for serious illnesses like good prolonged fevers with deliriums, good scarlet fevers, good plagues, good chronic dropsies, good pleurisies with inflammation of the lungs; that's what I like; that's where I triumph, and I wish, sir, you had every illness that I've just mentioned, that you had been abandoned by all doctors, crazy with despair, in the final agonies of death, that I might show you the excellence of my cures and the desire that I have to do you service.

ARGAN: Thank you very much, sir, for your kind wishes.

TOINETTE: Let me feel your pulse. (*Feels pulse.*) Come along now pulse, beat properly. Come on; I'll soon have you beating as you ought to. Good grief, this is a cheeky little pulse indeed. I can see clearly you don't know me yet – you naughty, naughty pulse. Who is your doctor?

ARGAN: M. Purgon.

TOINETTE: He's not on my list of great doctors. What does he say is wrong with you?

ARGAN: He says it's my liver; the others say it's my spleen.

TOINETTE: They're all nincompoops. It's your lungs!

ARGAN: My lungs?

TOINETTE: Yes! What are your symptoms?

ARGAN: From time to time I have headaches.

TOINETTE: Exactly! Your lungs!

ARGAN: Occasionally there seems to be a mist in front of my eyes.

TOINETTE: Your lungs!

ARGAN: Sometimes I have a pain in my heart.

TOINETTE: Your lungs!

ARGAN: Now and again all my limbs feel very tired.

TOINETTE: Your lungs!

ARGAN: And there are times I have pains in my stomach as if I had colic.

TOINETTE: Your lungs! Do you enjoy eating food?

ARGAN: Yes, sir.

TOINETTE: Your lungs! Do you like drinking wine?

ARGAN: Yes, sir.

TOINETTE: Your lungs! Do you appreciate a nice little nap after meals?

ARGAN: Yes, sir.

TOINETTE: Your lungs! Your lungs! I'm telling you, it's your lungs! What does your doctor advise you to eat?

ARGAN: He advises me to have soup.

TOINETTE: Nincompoop!

ARGAN: Poultry.

TOINETTE: Nincompoop!

ARGAN: Veal.

TOINETTE: Nincompoop!

ARGAN: Broth.

TOINETTE: Nincompoop!

ARGAN: Fresh eggs.

TOINETTE: Nincompoop!

ARGAN: A few prunes at night, to loosen the bowels.

TOINETTE: Nincompoop!

ARGAN: And, above all, to drink lots of water with my wine.

TOINETTE: Nincompoop! Nincompoopas! Nincompoopium! You must drink your wine undiluted, and, to thicken your blood, which is far too thin, you ought to eat lots of good fatty beef, good fatty pork, good Dutch cheese, porridge and rice puddings and chestnuts and waffles to strengthen and coagulate. Your doctor's a blockhead. I'm willing to come to see you from time to time while I'm staying here in this town.

ARGAN: I'm greatly obliged to you.

TOINETTE: What the devil are you doing with that arm?

ARGAN: What?

TOINETTE: If I were you, I'd have that arm cut off straight away.

ARGAN: Why?

TOINETTE: Don't you see that it's taking all the nourishment for itself? It's not giving the other one a chance to develop.

ARGAN: Yes, but I need my arm!

TOINETTE: If I were you, I'd also have that right eye removed.

ARGAN: My eye?

TOINETTE: Can't you understand that it's not good for the other one? It stops it from getting nourishment. Believe me, you'd better get rid of that right eye as soon as possible. You'll be able to see much more clearly with your left eye.

ARGAN: I'm sure it's not really urgent.

TOINETTE: Bye, bye. I'm sorry I have to leave you so soon but I've got an important consultation about a man who died yesterday.

ARGAN: About a man who died yesterday?

TOINETTE: Yes – to find out what should have been done to cure him. I'll see you soon. Bye, bye.

ARGAN: You know that I'm too sick to show you out.

BERALDE: Now that doctor really does seem to be a very clever man.

ARGAN: Yes, but he's a bit too quick for me.

BERALDE: All truly brilliant doctors are like that.

ARGAN: He'd cut off my arm and put out my eye to improve the other one. I don't think I want them to be improved. That would be a great operation, wouldn't it? I'd only have one arm. I'd be blind in one eye.

Scene 11

TOINETTE: (*Offstage.*) Come on now, that's enough of that! Please... Goodbye! (*Enters.*) I don't find that kind of thing very funny.

ARGAN: What's wrong?

TOINETTE: That doctor of yours wanted to... feel my pulse.

ARGAN: But... he's ninety.

BERALDE: Now brother, since your friend M. Purgon has fallen out with you, let me talk about the young man who has proposed to marry my niece.

ARGAN: No brother. I'm going to put her into a convent because she's stood in the way of my wishes. I can see quite clearly there's some intrigue at the bottom of all this. I'm certain of it. I've found out about a secret meeting.

BERALDE: Oh really brother, and if there was some little passion, would it be a crime? What harm can there be when it's all going to end in an honourable marriage?

ARGAN: That's all very well, brother, but she's going to be a nun, that's that!

BERALDE: You're only doing this to please... someone.

ARGAN: Go on! Say it! I know what you mean. It's my wife's name that sticks in your throat. You're always going on about her.

BERALDE: All right, brother, yes! Since I must speak freely I'll come straight to the point. I am talking about your wife. In the same way that I can't stand your obsession with medicine, I can't stand your obsession with her. I hate to see you fall headlong into all the traps she sets for you.

TOINETTE: Please don't talk about the mistress in that way, sir. She's above criticism, without deceit and she loves the master, oh yes, she loves him... no-one can imagine how much she loves him.

ARGAN: Tell him about all the affection she shows me.

TOINETTE: She does.

ARGAN: The worry that my sickness causes her.

TOINETTE: Indeed.

ARGAN: All the care and trouble she takes over me.

TOINETTE: It's a fact. (*To BERALDE.*) Let me prove it. Let me show you right here and now that my mistress loves her husband. (*To ARGAN.*) Sir, please allow me to show him just how wrong he is.

ARGAN: How?

TOINETTE: The mistress is just coming back. Stretch yourself out on that chair and pretend to be dead. You'll see how grieved she'll be when I tell her the news.

ARGAN: All right. I will.

TOINETTE: Be careful not to keep her distressed for too long. It might very well kill her.

ARGAN: Leave it to me.

TOINETTE: (*To BERALDE.*) Hide yourself in that corner.

ARGAN: Is there any risk involved in pretending to be dead?

TOINETTE: No, no, of course not. What risk could there be? Just stretch yourself out. (*Whispers.*) It'll be a pleasure to prove your brother wrong. Here's the mistress. Keep still.

BELINE enters.

Scene 12

TOINETTE: (*Crying out.*) Oh my God! Oh no! No! No! Oh, what a disaster.

BELINE: What is it, Toinette?

TOINETTE: Oh madam!

BELINE: What's wrong?

TOINETTE: Your husband is dead.

BELINE: My husband is dead?

TOINETTE: Yes, I'm afraid he is. The poor soul's dead and gone.

BELINE: Are you sure?

TOINETTE: I'm sure. No-one knows about it yet. I'm here on my own. He just passed away in my arms. Look, there he is stretched out in that chair.

BELINE: Well, thank heavens for that. That's a great weight off my shoulders. You're very silly, Toinette, to let yourself get upset just because he's dead.

TOINETTE: I thought, madam, that it was right to cry.

BELINE: Rubbish! He's not worth the trouble. Who's going to miss him? What earthly use was he to anybody? He was just a pest, untidy, disgusting, always having enemas or medicaments for his bowels, snivelling, coughing, always spitting, completely witless, irritating, bad-tempered, forever boring everyone and grumbling night and day at the maids and servants.

TOINETTE: What a splendid funeral oration.

BELINE: Toinette, you must help me carry out my plan and you can be sure that if you do help me you'll get a good reward. It's very lucky that no-one knows anything about this yet. Let's carry him to his bed and keep his death a secret until I've finished my business. I've got to get hold of certain papers and find some money. It's only fair! I deserve it after wasting the best years of my life with him. Come on Toinette, the first thing we've got to do is take all of his keys.

ARGAN: (*Getting up suddenly.*) Wait a minute.

BELINE: (*Surprised and terrified.*) Ahhhhhh!

ARGAN: Oh yes, my dearest wife. So that's how much you love me?

TOINETTE: Ahhh! The corpse is still alive.

ARGAN: (*To BELINE as she goes.*) I'm delighted to have seen how much you care for me. I'm delighted to have heard your touching tribute to me. Thank you very much for your advice. I'll be wise in the future. I'll never make the same mistakes again. (*BELINE has gone.*)

BERALDE: (*Coming from his hiding-place.*) Well brother, now you know.

TOINETTE: Upon my word, I'd never have believed it. Listen. I can hear your daughter coming. Lie down again and see how she'll take the news of your death. It's good to know these things and while you're at it, you might as well find out what your whole family thinks about you.

Scene 13

TOINETTE: (*Crying out.*) Oh heavens! Oh what a terrible thing to happen. What a dreadful day.

ANGELIQUE: What's wrong, Toinette? Why are you crying?

TOINETTE: Oh my God, I've got some terrible news for you.

ANGELIQUE: What is it?

TOINETTE: Your father's dead.

ANGELIQUE: My father's dead, Toinette?

TOINETTE: Yes. Look. There he is. It was so sudden. He had a kind of fainting fit and died.

ANGELIQUE: Oh heavens! This is unendurable, this is agonizing. Dear God, how could you allow this to happen? Why do I have to lose my father? Why do I have to lose the most precious thing I have in the world? And worse, why did I have to lose him when he was angry with me? What's going to happen to me? I'm ruined! Nothing can ever make up for this pernicious loss.

Scene 14

CLEANTE comes in.

CLEANTE: Angelique, my darling, tell me what's wrong. What's happened? Why are you crying?

ANGELIQUE: Oh Cleante, I'm crying because I've lost everything that's dear and precious in my life. My father is dead.

CLEANTE: Oh heavens, this is disastrous, this is catastrophic! Dear God, why did this have to happen now? I was coming to try to persuade him, with my own prayers and entreaties, to grant me my desire.

ANGELIQUE: Cleante, let's not talk about that any more. Let's forget all thought of marriage. After the loss of my father I don't want to live. I renounce the world forever. Yes, Daddy, if I stood in the way of some of your wishes, I will, at least, obey one of your requests and make up for the misery that I now accuse myself of having caused you. Oh Daddy, allow me to make my vow here, before you and let this kiss be a sign of my love and repentance.

ARGAN: (*Getting up.*) Oh my child!

ANGELIQUE: (*Frightened.*) Ahhh!

ARGAN: Come here. Don't be afraid. I'm not dead. You are truly my own flesh and blood, my natural daughter. I'm delighted to have heard your warm-hearted words.

ANGELIQUE: What a miracle! Daddy, since heaven, in its infinite goodness, has given you back to me and answered my prayers, let me fling myself at your feet and beg one favour of you. (*Falls on her knees.*) If you can't give me what my heart aches for, if you won't let me have Cleante for my husband, at least let me beg you not to force me to marry anyone else. That is the only thing I ask of you.

CLEANTE: (*Throws himself on his knees.*) Let her prayers and mine move you. Don't stand in the way of our love.

BERALDE: Brother, can you still refuse them?

TOINETTE: Oh sir, will you turn your back on love?

ARGAN: I will agree to the marriage – if he becomes a doctor. Yes, become a doctor and I'll give you my daughter.

CLEANTE: I will. Gladly! If that's the only thing I have to do to become your son-in-law of course I'll be a doctor, or even an apothecary or both if that's what you want! That's nothing! I'd do much more than that to win my dearest darling Angelique.

BERALDE: I've just had a brilliant idea, brother! Become a doctor yourself! It would be so convenient if you could provide yourself with everything you need.

TOINETTE: He's right! It's also the best way to get better quickly. Cure yourself. No illness would dare mess around with the doctor himself.

ARGAN: I think you're making fun of me brother. I'm too old to start studying.

BERALDE: Good lord, you won't have to study. You know enough about it already. There are many qualified doctors who know a lot less than you.

ARGAN: But you have to be able to speak Latin. You've got to know all about diseases and how to cure them.

BERALDE: When you get a doctor's cap and gown you will immediately know all about those things – you may even know more than you want to know.

ARGAN: What! Do you mean that when I put on the robes, I'll be able to talk about diseases?

BERALDE: Yes you will! All you have to do is put on the cap and gown, open your mouth and all nonsense becomes wisdom. All foolishness becomes logic. Would you like to become a doctor tonight?

ARGAN: What, now?

BERALDE: Yes. Here in your own house.

ARGAN: Here in my own house?

BERALDE: Yes – I've got some friends in the medical profession who would come over here at once to perform the ceremony here in your room. It won't cost you a thing.

ARGAN: But what do I have to say? What answers do I have to give?

BERALDE: They'll tell you what to do and they'll write down anything you have to say on a piece of paper. Go and put on your best clothes and I'll go and find my friends.

ARGAN: All right, I'll do it.

He exits.

CLEANTE: What's all this talk about having friends in the medical profession?

TOINETTE: What are you plotting?

BERALDE: Fun, just a little fun to finish off the evening. The actors are going to do a little divertissement about a doctor's graduation ceremony. I want us all to take part in the sketch and my brother will play the lead.

ANGELIQUE: I think you're making too much fun of Daddy.

BERALDE: No, Angelique, we're not making fun of him. We're only fulfilling his fantasies. It's just like the theatre. We'll all be playing parts. It'll be a laugh. After all, it's carnival time and we're allowed to let our hair down. Come on, let's find our costumes and get ready.

BERALDE and TOINETTE exeunt.

CLEANTE: (*To ANGELIQUE.*) Do you want to perform in this burlesque?

ANGELIQUE: Yes I do. It's my uncle's idea, so I'm happy to play my part.

The MUSICIAN and the LADY, already dressed and masked as stage doctors, come on with a clothes rail, a trunk or a basket of doctors costumes and masks, followed by BERALDE and TOINETTE.

MUSICIAN: Music!

Music plays.

Lights!

The lights begin to change.

Action!

The set begins to transform and the ACTORS put on their costumes and masks. When the music and change is completed, ARGAN enters.

BERALDE

Medignostic doctatores
Hippocratic professores
We see standing here before us
Homo sapiens molto glorious
Wish him wealth, bon appetitum
Hope no little fleas will eat 'm.
He would join our facultati
Be with us in corporati.
You must now his questionum
Top to toe examinonum.

MUSICIAN

I'd like this student to recite us
How he'd cure appendicitis!

ARGAN

Primus give some laxitiva,
Rhubarb, sennapods suprema
Douche the colon irritata.
Lastly, purge con enemata.

ALL (*Except ARGAN.*)

Bene, bene respondere
In nostro docto corpore
Bene, bene respondere

ACTRESS

What heals chronic emphysema
Whooping cough and scarlatina?

ARGAN

Primus give some laxitiva
Rhubarb, sennapods suprema
Douche the colon irritata.
Lastly, purge con enemata.

ALL (*Except ARGAN.*)

Bene, bene respondere
In nostro docto corpore
Bene, bene respondere

CLEANTE

What's the cure for laryngitis
Cholera and hepatitis?

ARGAN

Primus give some laxitiva
Rhubarb, sennapods suprema
Douche the colon irritata.
Lastly, purge con enemata.

LADY

Would this student care to mention
How he'd deal with hypertension?

ARGAN

Primus give some laxitiva
Rhubarb, sennapods suprema
Douche the colon irritata.
Lastly, purge con enemata.

ALL (*Except ARGAN.*)

Bene, bene respondere
In nostro docto corpore
Bene, bene respondere

TOINETTE

Can you tell us without lying
Do you have a cure for dying?

Everybody gasps.

ARGAN (*After a pause.*)

Primus give some laxitiva
Rhubarb, sennapods suprema
Douche the colon irritata.
Lastly, purge con enemata.

ALL (*Except ARGAN.*)

Bene, bene respondere
In nostro docto corpore
Bene, bene respondere

BERALDE

Swear that you will keep our rule
To treat each patient like a fool.

ALL (*Except ARGAN.*)

Swear! Swear! Swear! Swear!

ARGAN

I swear.

BERALDE

By the powers bestowed on me
From this moment you will be
Master of medicine
Prefect of purging
Bachelor of bleeding
Laureate of lancing
And Doctor of death.

The rest of the COMPANY approach ARGAN and put on his cap and gown, singing.

ALL

Bene, bene respondere
In nostro docto corpore
Bene, bene respondere

ARGAN: Doctors of this great profession, I'm lost for
words. Let me try to express what I feel. This is the
happiest moment of my life. No mere words can
describe my emotions. To presume that I could ever
thank you would be as foolish as to attempt to give light
to the sun, fish to the sea or roses to the spring. I am
now a doctor! I am now a doctor! Thank you! Thank
you! Thank you! You have made me the happiest man
in the world. I feel young. I feel like a child. This joy
I feel will last for the rest of my life. I am transported!!

The COMPANY lift him up and sing.

ALL (*Except ARGAN.*)

Long life, long life, Doctor novum
We hear your words of wisdom
May you eat, drink, bleed and killum
Amen, amen.

The curtain falls.

THE END.

GEORGE DANDIN

in a new version by Ranjit Bolt

Characters

GEORGE DANDIN,
a cuckold

LUBIN,
a hired man

M. DE SOTENVILLE,
George Dandin's father-in-law

CLITANDRE,
a young nobleman

ANGELIQUE,
George Dandin's wife, in love with Clitandre

CLAUDINE,
Angélique's maid

COLIN,
George Dandin's servant

George Dandin was first performed by Red Shift Theatre Company on the 9th of February 1995 at Darlington Arts Centre with the following cast:

GEORGE DANDIN, Malcolm Ridley

LUBIN, Simon Hunt

M. DE SOTENVILLE, Jeff Bellamy

CLITANDRE, Gareth Tyrrell

ANGELIQUE, Sally Giles

CLAUDINE, Stephanie Woodcraft

DIRECTION, Jonathan Holloway

ACT ONE

GEORGE DANDIN: You know, it's no joke having an
aristocrat for a wife. My marriage is an excellent lesson
for any ordinary bloke who's thinking of rising above his
station: don't marry a nobleman's daughter! I grant you,
titles are all right in themselves – they're certainly not to
be sneezed at. But when all's said and done they bring so
much trouble with them, you'd be better off not touching
one with a barge-pole. I've found that out to my cost:
I know how the nobility carry on once they've taken
one of us so-called ordinary people into their family.
It's not really you they're marrying – it's your money,
and everything that goes with it. If you want my opinion,
rich as I am, I'd have been much better off marrying into
a good, honest country family than taking a wife who
thinks I'm beneath her; who considers it an indignity to
share my name; and thinks that even if I was as rich as
Croesus, I could never be a good enough husband for
her. I married for love and where's it got me? I'm being
exploited. I've lavished all my affection on Angélique,
and what's she given me in return? Sod all. She walks all
over me, the little bitch. She even belts me one from
time to time. (Not that I don't give as good as I get in
that department.) I can't take much more of it. I'm at the
end of my tether. And as if all that weren't enough, I'm
beginning to suspect her of infidelity. A young vicomte's
moved in over the way. Good looking bastard! I've seen
him eyeing her up. It's only a matter of time now. One
day I'll come home and find them in bed together.
Hmmmm... I should have seen it coming. George
Dandin, George Dandin, what a prize ass you've been!
My house is just a living hell these days. I can't set foot
in it without something or someone giving me grief.

Enter LUBIN.

GEORGE DANDIN: (*Seeing LUBIN come out of the house.*)
What in God's name is that clown doing coming out of
my house?

LUBIN: Who's that man? He's looking at me.

GEORGE DANDIN: He obviously doesn't know me.

LUBIN: I reckon he suspects something.

GEORGE DANDIN: Hm. He doesn't seem in any hurry to
say "Hello".

LUBIN: I'm afraid he might say he saw me coming out of
here.

GEORGE DANDIN: Ahem! Good day to you.

LUBIN: Your servant, monsieur.

GEORGE DANDIN: You're not from around here, are you?

LUBIN: What if I'm not?

GEORGE DANDIN: Nothing. (*Beat.*) But you're not, are
you?

LUBIN: That's right – I'm not. I'm only here for tomorrow's
fair. Not that it's any business of yours.

GEORGE DANDIN: (*Aside.*) We've got a deep one here.
(*Aloud.*) Tell me, monsieur...?

LUBIN: Lubin's the name. Not that it's any...

GEORGE DANDIN: All right, all right – relax, can't you?
Tell me, monsieur Lubin, would I be right in thinking
that you've just come out of there. (*Points at his front door.*)

LUBIN: Ssshh!

GEORGE DANDIN: Eh?

LUBIN: Be quiet!

GEORGE DANDIN: What is it? What's the matter?

LUBIN: Mum's the word! You mustn't say you saw me.

GEORGE DANDIN: Why the Devil not?

LUBIN: Christ almighty! Because... (*Stops.*)

GEORGE DANDIN: Because what?

LUBIN: Talk softly, can't you? I'm afraid someone might hear us.

GEORGE DANDIN: Who? Where? Don't be so stupid.

LUBIN: Well you see, it's like this: I've just been speaking to the mistress of the house, on behalf of a certain gentleman who fancies her. No one's supposed to find out about it... if you catch my drift. (*Winks.*)

GEORGE DANDIN: I think I'm beginning to, yes.

LUBIN: You see the thing is, he said I wasn't to let myself be seen. So for God's sake don't mention this to a living soul. It's more than my job's worth.

GEORGE DANDIN: Don't you worry about a thing. My lips are sealed.

LUBIN: I want to do things secretly, see? Just like I was told.

GEORGE DANDIN: Quite right too. But don't worry – I'm the soul of discretion. Your secret's safe with me. Continue...

LUBIN: By all accounts the husband's jealous – not to say dangerous. According to the maid, he hits her – and her mistress. In fact, not to put too fine a point on it, he's one of the most sadistic bastards you could ever hope to meet. He'd go apeshit if he found out someone was seducing his wife. D'you follow?

GEORGE DANDIN: Only too well.

LUBIN: And if he does find out there'll be Hell to pay.

GEORGE DANDIN: No doubt.

LUBIN: They want to deceive him very discreetly. You do see that?

GEORGE DANDIN: I think that point *has* sunk in, thank you.

LUBIN: The fact is, if you were to say you'd spotted me coming out of his house, you'd spoil everything. Are you with me?

GEORGE DANDIN: Absolutely. Now, if you wouldn't mind telling me what's going on. To begin with, the person who sent you here – what's his name?

LUBIN: It's... Here. Hang on a minute – what are you asking all these questions for? What's your game?

GEORGE DANDIN: Game? I don't know what you're talking about. I'm naturally curious, that's all.

LUBIN: I see. Well, he happens to be top cat where I come from: the Vicomte de... de... damn, I'm sorry – I can never for the life of me remember his title. Anyway, his name's Clitandre.

GEORGE DANDIN: Is he that stylish young courtier who lives...?

LUBIN: Over by those trees? That's right.

GEORGE DANDIN: (*Aside.*) So that's it! That's why he's come to live on top of me. Why else would he have chosen this spot? I had my suspicions, and it seems they're justified. (*Aloud.*) Tell me more.

LUBIN: To be honest, monsieur, I don't really see why I should. I'm still not happy about this. Just why exactly do you want to know about him?

GEORGE DANDIN: I told you, I'm naturally curious. For Pete's sake man, what's your problem? What are you getting so uptight about?

LUBIN: Uptight! Who's getting uptight? I'll tell you this much: he's the most generous man you're ever likely to meet. He gave me three gold pieces just to go and tell the woman he's in love with her, and that he'd give anything for the honour of speaking to her. Don't you think it was good of him to pay me so well? I mean to say, compare three gold pieces with the ten sous I get for a day's work.

GEORGE DANDIN: (*Aside.*) It's as plain as the nose on my face! This fellow's a pimp – and Angélique's the... Oh, God! What am I going to do? I must try and find out more. (*Aloud.*) So, did you deliver your message?

LUBIN: Yes. I found a girl called Claudine there. She understood at once what I wanted, and arranged for me to speak to her mistress. She's one Hell of a bright spark, she is. I've never met a maid with such brains.

GEORGE DANDIN: (*Aside.*) Ah! The little baggage! I'll flay her alive when I get her alone!

LUBIN: She's pretty, too – a real peach – that Claudine. I've fallen for her. She's only got to say the word, and I'd marry her like a shot. Mind you, I doubt if I could keep up with her. She's a real goer by the looks of her. And as for brains, well – like I said – she leaves me in the starting blocks.

GEORGE DANDIN: Yes, yes – I think I've got the picture. Tell me, what answer did her mistress give this monsieur Clitandre? Is she prepared to welcome his... advances?

LUBIN: She told me to say... hang on, I'm not sure I can remember all of it... that she's very grateful to him for loving her and so on, but because her husband's such a thug, he'll have to... what was it?... proceed with the utmost caution, and think of some stratagem so they can meet. That was the gist of it, at any rate.

GEORGE DANDIN: (*Aside.*) The shameless little slut! I'll throttle her!

LUBIN: Wouldn't it be bloody hilarious, though? The husband wouldn't have a clue what was going on. Serve him right, too, the jealous old git! I mean to say, what does he expect if he treats his wife like a human punch-bag?

GEORGE DANDIN: He does?

LUBIN: Goodbye. And remember, not a word to anyone. We wouldn't want the old sod finding out about all this, now, would we?

GEORGE DANDIN: No, of course we wouldn't.

LUBIN: As for me, I won't give the game away. I'm a sly old devil. Nobody's going to know what I've been up to. (*Goes.*)

GEORGE DANDIN

So, she's been carrying on behind my back –
I'm married to a nymphomaniac –
A bitch on heat who's ready to... you know
With the first dog who sniffs her. Frankly, though
What makes the situation ten times worse
Is this: that damned nobility of hers
Means I'm unable to retaliate –
My hands are tied. I should have picked a mate
From my own kind – a country girl. "Oh, yes?"
I hear you ask. "Would she be any less
Inclined to find herself a lover?" No.
I could have thrashed her senseless for it, though!

Instead I chose a lady. If I tried
Some rough stuff on her I'd be crucified.
Her father would be on to me at once,
The proud, pretentious, puffed up, pompous ponce!
Why did I marry this... this whore? God knows.
I wanted to be pissed on, I suppose.
Christ! I could kick myself. I'm furious. What?
Has she no shame at all? No, clearly not,
If she's arranging meetings with young men.
I may not get a chance like this again.
Her father must be found immediately.
I have to show him how she's treating me.
I can't get back at her until I do,
That much is certain. Here he comes, on cue!

Enter M. DE SOTENVILLE.

M. DE SOTENVILLE: What is it, son-in-law? You seem upset.

GEORGE DANDIN: I am, and with good reason. If you knew what I'd just found out. It's a scandal. An absolute bloody...

M. DE SOTENVILLE: Good Heavens, son-in-law! Where are your manners? You must bow to your betters when you approach them. How many times must I upbraid you for your slipshod behaviour?

GEORGE DANDIN: (*Aside.*) Jesus! Didn't I tell you he was pompous? (*Aloud.*) Believe me, father-in-law I had other things on my mind, or...

M. DE SOTENVILLE: There you go again! Why do you choose to remain so stubbornly ignorant of the world and its ways? Will I never be able to teach you how to conduct yourself in the presence of persons of quality?

GEORGE DANDIN: You what?

M. DE SOTENVILLE: When will you learn to stop being so familiar? On no account are you to call me

"father-in-law". It is far too informal. Can you not
accustom yourself to addressing me as "monsieur"?
I don't expect much from a provincial upstart, but you
might at least attempt some sort of nod, however feeble,
in the direction of civilized behaviour.

GEORGE DANDIN: What the Hell are you...?! Look, if
you call me "son-in-law", why on earth shouldn't I call
you "father-in-law"?

M. DE SOTENVILLE: Why, for a whole host of reasons.
The cases are not the same. You must understand that
you have no right to address a person of my rank in that
manner. You may be my son-in-law but there is a vast
difference between us. You must have a clearer sense of
who and what you are. Let me make this plain once and
for all: you have been granted the enormous privilege
of forming an alliance with the house of de Sotenville.
I was prepared to overlook your, to say the least,
questionable social credentials. But I am not a man
to forgo one jot of what he's entitled to. Moreover,
(*Menacingly.*) I have always gone to great lengths to prove
it. That being so, you would be well advised to treat me
with more respect. Always remember that you owe your
present, enviable position to two things: your love for
our daughter and my democratic inclinations.

GEORGE DANDIN: Aren't you forgetting something?

M. DE SOTENVILLE: If you are referring to your – ahem!
– qualifications...

GEORGE DANDIN: I'm referring to my money.
"Qualifications" my arse!

M. DE SOTENVILLE: Dandin...

GEORGE DANDIN: You're incapable of admitting it,
aren't you?

M. DE SOTENVILLE: Admitting what?

GEORGE DANDIN: Your motives were entirely mercenary.

M. DE SOTENVILLE: I haven't the least idea what you're talking about. And I'll thank you not to be so vulgar. Money is not something one discusses in polite society. Really, son–in–law, you must know your place. I am not about to give up mine, and your marrying into my family doesn't change things in the least. A spade, in other words, is still a spade. But I've given you a little warning – that's enough. Now, tell me what's troubling you. If you have a legitimate grievance, I shall do my level best to see that you obtain redress. On that you have my solemn word as a gentleman.

GEORGE DANDIN: You want me to come right out with it? All right then, get this, monsieur de Sotenville: I have grounds for thinking that...

M. DE SOTENVILLE: Be careful, son-in-law. It is extremely disrespectful to call your betters by their surnames. I should have thought you would have got that into your head by now. God knows I've had occasion to speak to you about it often enough! You should address me as "monsieur" – nothing more or less.

GEORGE DANDIN: Very well then, monsieur. Nothing-more-or-less, I'm here to tell you that my wife has...

M. DE SOTENVILLE: Stop! You must learn not to refer to my daughter as "my wife". Now, let's start again.

GEORGE DANDIN: I'm fed up with this. Are you trying to tell me my wife's not my wife?

M. DE SOTENVILLE: Certainly, she is your wife. You are not permitted to call her that, however – although, certainly, you might have done so with impunity, had you been her equal.

GEORGE DANDIN: Is that so? Then what the Devil *am* I "permitted" to call her? (*Aside.*) Ah! George Dandin! What have you done? (*To M. DE SOTENVILLE.*) Do you think you could forget your nobility for a split second and let me speak to you man to man? To Hell with all this protocol. I'm telling you, I'm not happy with my marriage.

M. DE SOTENVILLE: Your exquisite reason, son-in-law? How can you possibly be so upset over something that has brought you so many advantages?

GEORGE DANDIN: What advantages... *monsieur*... since that's what I'm supposed to call you? It's not as if you've lost by it yourself. You'll excuse me for saying this, but without me your affairs would be in a total mess. I need hardly point out that my money papered over some pretty yawning cracks. I've never seen such extravagance. You get through cash at a simply incredible rate – then expect me to pick up the bills. And as if that weren't enough, you never lose an opportunity to humiliate me. Well it's just not fair. I'm sick and tired of it, I really am.

M. DE SOTENVILLE: You go too far.

GEORGE DANDIN: I mean, I spend my life bailing you out of scrapes, and what do I get in return? Nothing.

M. DE SOTENVILLE: You call it nothing to be allied to the de Sotenvilles? Why, thanks to us your sons will be gentlemen. You should count yourself honoured. Nor can you pretend that your marriage hasn't raised your status among your plebean friends. Not to mention the fact that it has undoubtedly helped you in your business. And another thing...

GEORGE DANDIN: Excellent! My sons will be gentlemen, and I'll be a cuckold – unless you do something about it, that is. Your daughter is not honourable, monsieur.

M. DE SOTENVILLE: Angélique not honourable! How dare you even hint at such a thing? There had better be some foundation for this outrageous allegation.

GEORGE DANDIN: Oh, there's plenty of foundation for it. Angélique is not behaving as a wife ought to behave, and that's putting it mildly. She's doing things that threaten your honour.

M. DE SOTENVILLE: Be careful, Dandin. My daughter comes from a respectable family and would never do anything that might cause her virtue to be questioned. I can claim with some satisfaction that it is more than three hundred years since a de Sotenville gave her husband the least grounds for complaint: our women are as chaste as our men are courageous. There was a Jacqueline de Sotenville who refused to be the mistress of a duke, even though he was a peer of the realm and governor of our province, and certainly had plenty to offer.

GEORGE DANDIN: And why should I give a damn about that?

M. DE SOTENVILLE: There was a Mathurine de Sotenville who refused twenty thousand ecus that were offered her by a favourite of the king, merely for the privilege of speaking to her.

GEORGE DANDIN: Really? Well, your daughter's not quite so choosy – not now she's married to me, at any rate. She's become – how can I put this? – more... friendly? And if you'd only give me a chance to tell you what I've just discovered, you might be a little more sympathetic.

M. DE SOTENVILLE: Explain yourself, son-in-law. Angélique may be my daughter, but I am not the man to defend her, should it transpire that she has indeed behaved as you suggest. On the contrary, I shall be the first to punish her. You can count on me. I treat questions of honour with the utmost seriousness. I am an aristocrat. My reputation means more to me than anything else in the world – more even than life itself. But Angélique has been brought up as strictly as any girl in France. I should be utterly astonished – not to say horrified – to learn of any – how shall I put it? – lapse on her part.

GEORGE DANDIN: All I know is, there's a young vicomte here (you've seen him) who's trying to seduce her under my very nose. She knows he's after her and she doesn't seem to be raising many objections.

M. DE SOTENVILLE: I swear to God, if she's lost her honour I shall strangle her with my bare hands – and her lover. Or, at the very least, he'll make some recompense.

GEORGE DANDIN: You know my grievance. I demand satisfaction.

M. DE SOTENVILLE: Don't upset yourself. Rest assured, you shall have it from them both. I'm not the sort of man who lets things lie. But are you really certain of your facts?

GEORGE DANDIN: Quite certain.

M. DE SOTENVILLE: Take care. As a commoner, you couldn't possibly be expected to understand this, but there are ticklish matters between gentlemen such as the Vicomte and myself. There should be no mistakes in an affair of this kind. I could not possibly afford to offend a fellow aristocrat, when he had given me no grounds for doing so. Moreover, as I've already said, I find it hard to believe that a daughter of mine would show you anything less than the respect you deserve.

GEORGE DANDIN: Then it's a good job everything I've told you is true. (*He calls into the house.*) Claudine! Tell your mistress to come out here.

M. DE SOTENVILLE: Well, it is a terrible blow, I must
say. To think that Angélique could behave in such a
despicable fashion, after the excellent example her
mother and I have set her. I must get to the bottom of
this at once. Follow me, son-in-law, and above all keep
calm. And then we'd better go and find that vicomte.
You shall see how I act when my nearest and dearest
are meddled with.

GEORGE DANDIN: Here he comes now.

Enter CLITANDRE.

M. DE SOTENVILLE: Monsieur, do you know who I am?

CLITANDRE: Not as far as I'm aware, monsieur.

M. DE SOTENVILLE: I am the baron de Sotenville.

CLITANDRE: Good for you.

M. DE SOTENVILLE: My name is well known at court and
I had the honour, in my youth, of distinguishing myself
among the pick of the officers of the Arrière-Ban at
Nancy.

CLITANDRE: Well done.

M. DE SOTENVILLE: Monsieur, my father Jean-Gilles de
Sotenville, was privileged to be present in person at the
great siege of Montauban.

CLITANDRE: Delighted to hear it.

M. DE SOTENVILLE: My grandfather, baron Bertrand de
Sotenville, reached so exalted a position that he was
permitted to sell all his property in order to raise a
regiment for the crown.

CLITANDRE: I don't doubt it, monsieur, and of course I'm
extremely impressed. But I can't help wondering what all
this has to do with me.

M. DE SOTENVILLE: It has come to my notice, monsieur, that you are philandering with a certain young person – to wit my daughter. I need hardly say that I take an interest in her, and in this gentleman, who has the honour of being my son-in-law.

CLITANDRE: Philandering with your daughter? Me? Monsieur...

M. DE SOTENVILLE: Yes, you. I'm very glad to have this opportunity of speaking to you. Would you be so good as to shed some light on this affair? If there is any truth in what I've been told, I shall of course be obliged to act accordingly.

CLITANDRE: Well, fortunately you've been misinformed. Who did you hear this monstrous slander from?

M. DE SOTENVILLE: Someone who feels he has ample grounds for believing it.

CLITANDRE: That "someone" has been lying to you. I am an honourable man. Do you think me capable of such a despicable action? What? Pursue a girl who has the honour of being the daughter of the baron de Sotenville! I respect you far too much even to contemplate such a thing. Whoever told you this is an imbecile.

M. DE SOTENVILLE: Well, son-in-law...?

GEORGE DANDIN: Well what?

CLITANDRE: He's a scoundrel, I tell you. An absolute swine.

M. DE SOTENVILLE: (*To DANDIN.*) Answer him.

GEORGE DANDIN: Answer him yourself.

CLITANDRE: If I had the remotest idea who he was, I'd run him through, in front of you.

M. DE SOTENVILLE: (*To DANDIN.*) You must support your story.

GEORGE DANDIN: What do you mean, support it? It doesn't need supporting. It's true.

CLITANDRE: Monsieur, am I to understand that it is your son-in-law who...?

M. DE SOTENVILLE: Complained to me of this? Indeed it is.

CLITANDRE: In that case he should be thanking God for the privilege of being related to you. If he weren't I'd teach him to say things like that about a man of my rank.

Enter ANGELIQUE and CLAUDINE.

GEORGE DANDIN: As luck would have it, here comes Angélique. I dare say *she* can clear this matter up.

CLITANDRE: Then it was you, madame, who told your husband I was in love with you?

ANGELIQUE: Me! Why would I tell him that? Are you? I wish you were. I'd be only too delighted if you chose me. You're welcome to try your best. Go ahead, and with my blessing. Use every trick in the book: send me messages; write me secret love letters; they'll be well received. I mean it. Oh, and another thing: I'd advise you to find out when my husband won't be in, or when I'll be out walking. That way we can meet, and you can talk love to me. You've only to come and visit me and I promise you, you'll get a warmer welcome than you might expect. Mind you, if you knew what I had to put up with from this monster every day of my life, you wouldn't be surprised at all.

CLITANDRE: Hey! Calm down, madame. There's no need to tell me all this, or to get so worked up. I haven't the slightest intention of pursuing you. But who the Devil told you that I had?

ANGELIQUE: No one. I only just got here. And I'm not in the least worked up, thank you very much. It's you men who are losing your cool. I haven't the foggiest idea what all this hoo-ha is about.

CLITANDRE: For my part, madame, people can say what they like, but you know whether I spoke of love to you when we met. As I've just told your father, I am an honourable man. I'm not in the habit of philandering with women. Certainly not with women of your evident breeding.

ANGELIQUE: If only you had done. You wouldn't have regretted it, I can assure you.

CLITANDRE: Hm. Yes. Well, be that as it may, I'm not about to do so. I'm not a man to cause a lady any alarm.

ANGELIQUE: Alarm! Who said anything about alarm?

CLITANDRE: Please, madame, I believe I've made my position clear, and I see no reason for prolonging this discussion. I have too much respect for you, and for your parents, to contemplate attempting to see you in secret, let alone seduce you.

M. DE SOTENVILLE: Well, there's your satisfaction, son-in-law. What do you say?

GEORGE DANDIN: I say it's a load of bloody rubbish. I know what I know. What's more, since you force me to say it, she got a message from him just now.

ANGELIQUE: I got a message?

CLITANDRE: I sent a message?

ANGELIQUE: Claudine...

CLITANDRE: Mademoiselle, am I to understand that you're in a position to refute this allegation?

CLAUDINE: That's right, I am. It's a pack of lies from beginning to end. My master's off his head and no mistake.

GEORGE DANDIN: Hold your tongue, hussy! I know exactly what you've been up to. You were the one who let the messenger in just now.

CLAUDINE: Who? Me?

GEORGE DANDIN: Yes. You. There's no need to look as though butter wouldn't melt in your mouth.

CLAUDINE: I don't know what the world's coming to. To suspect me of all people! I'm a good girl, I am.

GEORGE DANDIN: That's enough out of you, you crafty little bitch! I'm just sport to you, aren't I? You take advantage of my good nature. You could hunt from one end of France to the other and you wouldn't find a kinder master than me. All right, perhaps I beat you now and then, but only when you've really asked for it.

CLAUDINE: (*To ANGELIQUE.*) Madame, I appeal to you: did I...?

GEORGE DANDIN: I said shut up. You can pay for their pranks as well as your own: it's not as if *your* father was a gentleman. I may not be able to teach you a lesson out here, but it'll be a different story in the privacy of my own home. You're going to regret this, I promise you.

CLAUDINE: Oh, yes? And what are you planning on doing? Eh?

GEORGE DANDIN: One more insolent word out of you and I'll dismiss you on the spot.

CLAUDINE: Dismiss me! Huh! You wouldn't have the nerve!

GEORGE DANDIN: How dare you talk to me like that! I've had just about as much as I can take from you... you... (*Moves towards her, menacing.*)

CLAUDINE: (*Hides behind CLITANDRE.*) Help, monsieur!

GEORGE DANDIN: (*Stops short and clutches his chest.*) Ooh! My heart!

M. DE SOTENVILLE: Really, Dandin, you must learn to control that temper of yours. It'll be the death of you one of these days. I say! Are you all right?

GEORGE DANDIN: I'll be fine in a minute.

CLAUDINE: Serves him right for behaving like a barbarian. I hope it kills him one of these days!

M. DE SOTENVILLE: Perhaps we could return to the business in hand.

ANGELIQUE: Quite right, father. What can I say? It's such a monstrous, such an utterly unfounded accusation – it hurts me so much – I can scarcely bring myself to answer it. It's intolerable to be accused by one's husband when one hasn't even done anything. To be humiliated in front of everyone like this. (*To DANDIN.*) But I suppose it's just another of those crosses one has to bear in the name of love.

CLAUDINE: You see how virtuous she is. It makes my heart bleed to see that bastard treating her the way he does. And it doesn't stop there, either. I could tell you a thing or two.

ANGELIQUE: Not now Claudine, please. I've learned to live with it. (*Sighing.*) No – my problem's not infidelity – it's the opposite. If only I *were* capable of welcoming a man's advances. Goodbye! I'm going. I can't stand any more of this. It's an outrage, that's what it is. I've had enough. I want to be alone! (*She makes a melodramatic exit.*)

M. DE SOTENVILLE: See that? You don't deserve the wife I've given you – so virtuous, so long-suffering.

CLAUDINE: Jesus Christ! Want to know what I think? It'd serve him right if she did it – what he says she's done. I wouldn't think twice about it if I was in her shoes. (*To CLITANDRE.*) I mean it, monsieur: you should punish him; you must punish him; you must make love to my mistress. I'm telling you, go for it! It's time someone did. What's more I'll help you, since he's already blown me up for it. It'll serve him right for making our lives a misery. Mind you, when all's said and done the only place for someone like him's an asylum. (*Goes.*)

M. DE SOTENVILLE: Son-in-law, all this is no more than you deserve. You have set everyone against you. No wonder they say such things about you. It's really high time you learned how to treat a lady of quality. Let me make this absolutely clear: there must be no more episodes like this. And another thing. I find it impossible to believe that you could raise your hand to a sweet, docile creature like Angélique, but if I ever find out that you have, I shan't be answerable for what I do.

GEORGE DANDIN: Even when I'm in the right I'm in the wrong! It's bloody infuriating! These people will be the death of me!

CLITANDRE: (*To M. DE SOTENVILLE*) Monsieur, you see how I have been falsely accused. You're a man who knows all about points of honour: I demand satisfaction for the affront I have suffered.

M. DE SOTENVILLE: Quite right. Etiquette requires no less. Come, son-in-law, you heard the gentleman: give him the satisfaction he demands.

GEORGE DANDIN: Satisfaction? It seems to me that that's already been taken care of.

M. DE SOTENVILLE: You have accused him falsely. The rules of honour demand that you give him some redress.

GEORGE DANDIN: I don't agree. I haven't accused him falsely. I'm entitled to my opinion, aren't I? Or is it one law for the nobility and another for the rest of us?

M. DE SOTENVILLE: Your opinion is utterly irrelevant. He has denied your accusation. That should be satisfaction enough for you. Furthermore, you have no proof. And most importantly of all, the Vicomte is your social superior and, by definition, in the right.

GEORGE DANDIN: Let's just see if I've got this straight. You mean to say that, if I found him in bed with my wife he could clear himself simply by denying it?

M. DE SOTENVILLE: No arguments, please. You have no option but to apologise. I shall tell you what to say.

GEORGE DANDIN: Me apologise to him! After what he...

M. DE SOTENVILLE: Come on, son–in–law. Stop messing about! I haven't got all day. You needn't worry about overdoing it, since I shall be directing you.

GEORGE DANDIN: But how could I possibly...? I mean to say, it simply...!

M. DE SOTENVILLE: For Heaven's sake, son-in-law, don't make me lose my temper or I shall take the Vicomte's side. Now, if you'd be so good as to repeat after me...

GEORGE DANDIN: Ah! George Dandin!

M. DE SOTENVILLE: Cap in hand first, please. How many times must I tell you these things? The Vicomte is a gentleman – you're not. And you can kneel while you're about it.

GEORGE DANDIN: Jesus H. Christ!

M. DE SOTENVILLE: I won't tell you again, Dandin. (*DANDIN kneels.*) Now, if you're ready: "Monsieur."

GEORGE DANDIN: Monsieur.

M. DE SOTENVILLE: (*Seeing that DANDIN is reluctant.*) "I ask your pardon."

GEORGE DANDIN: I ask your pardon.

M. DE SOTENVILLE: "For the unworthy suspicions I have entertained of you."

GEORGE DANDIN: For the unworthy suspicions I have entertained of you.

M. DE SOTENVILLE: "The reason was that I had not had the honour of knowing you..."

GEORGE DANDIN: The reason was that I had not had the honour of knowing you...

M. DE SOTENVILLE: "... And I beg you to believe..."

GEORGE DANDIN: ... And I beg you to believe...

M. DE SOTENVILLE: "That I am and shall always remain..."

GEORGE DANDIN: That I am and shall always remain...

M. DE SOTENVILLE: "Your humble and devoted servant."

GEORGE DANDIN: Humble and devoted servant! The bastard wants to cuckold me!

M. DE SOTENVILLE: Ah!

CLITANDRE: Monsieur le baron, really, that's enough.

M. DE SOTENVILLE: No, monsieur le Vicomte, it is not. I want him to finish. Everything must be done by the book. "That I am your humble and devoted servant."

GEORGE DANDIN: That I am your humble and devoted servant.

CLITANDRE: And I'm yours, monsieur, I assure you – with all my heart. Please – why don't we just forget the whole affair. (*To M. DE SOTENVILLE.*) And as for you, monsieur de Sotenville, I bid you good day and I'm sorry for any inconvenience you may have suffered.

M. DE SOTENVILLE: I kiss your hands, monsieur le Vicomte, and if you should ever feel in the mood for some sport, you're welcome to come and course a hare with me whenever you like.

CLITANDRE: You're too kind, monsieur. (*Goes.*)

M. DE SOTENVILLE: There you are, son-in-law: that's the
way to get things done.

Goodbye. Permit me to inform you that you have
entered a family that will protect you, and will not allow
you to be insulted in any way. (*Goes.*)

GEORGE DANDIN

Dandin, you've only got your just deserts.
And yet it isn't that that really hurts:
What rankles is the way that Angélique
Managed to conjure up a fit of pique
Just now. Yes, far from being the slightest bit
Ashamed of what she's done, she's proud of it!
If this goes on, and I don't get my way
I swear to God on high, I'm going to flay
The hide off her, the shameless little whore.
Damn! What the Hell did I get married for?
These people's prime, if not their sole concern,
Is to make me look a fool at every turn.
I fail to see how things could get much worse.
Christ, what an imbecile I've been! I curse
The day I came across that family:
I mean to say, what have they done for me?
Made me a total laughing-stock, that's what;
Robbed me of any dignity I'd got.
Well, I'm not going to take this lying down:
I'm tired of being treated like a clown.
Her father holds the key: what I must do
Is make him see that what I've said is true;
What's more, I'm certain I can find a way –
Even this dog is going to have his day.

ACT TWO

CLAUDINE, LUBIN.

CLAUDINE: I guessed it came from you.

LUBIN: I swear I only said a word or two to someone, in passing. I didn't want him to tell anyone he'd seen me coming out of the house. People round here must be terrible gossips.

CLAUDINE: The Vicomte certainly chose well when he made you his messenger! You're a complete and utter cretin.

LUBIN: Next time I'll be more careful.

CLAUDINE: I should bloody well hope so.

LUBIN: Let's change the subject. Listen...

CLAUDINE: To what?

LUBIN: Turn your face a bit towards me.

CLAUDINE: All right. Now, what is it?

LUBIN: Claudine.

CLAUDINE: Hmm?

LUBIN: Come on – you must know what I'm going to say. (*CLAUDINE shakes her head.*) For Pete's sake! I'm dying for you.

CLAUDINE: You are?

LUBIN: Yes, damn it, I am! You must believe me.

CLAUDINE: What if I do?

LUBIN: My heart starts thumping when I look at you.

CLAUDINE: I'm glad to hear it.

LUBIN: What did you do to be so beautiful?

CLAUDINE: Nothing special.

LUBIN: Look, let's not beat about the bush: we can be married if you want.

CLAUDINE: You might be jealous like my master.

LUBIN: I won't.

CLAUDINE: I hate suspicious husbands. I want one who trusts me; who's so sure of my chastity he could see me surrounded by men and not turn a hair.

LUBIN: Well, that's how I'll be.

CLAUDINE: It's utterly moronic to be jealous of your wife and torment her, the way *he* does. What's the use of it? It only gives us ideas. Husbands often dig their own graves by making scenes.

LUBIN: All right: I'll let you do whatever you like.

CLAUDINE: Then you're certain not to be deceived. When a husband gives us a free hand, we behave ourselves. It's like someone opening his purse and saying: "Take!" You never take more than you should. But if people are mean with you, you go out of your way to rip them off.

LUBIN: Then I'll be one of the ones who opens his purse. Now, all you've got to do is marry me.

CLAUDINE: We'll see; we'll see.

LUBIN: Come here, then.

CLAUDINE: What do you want?

LUBIN: Just come here.

CLAUDINE: Steady! You're in too much of a hurry.

He lunges at her.

LUBIN: Come on! Why so unfriendly?

He grabs her and tries to fondle her breasts. She pushes him away.

CLAUDINE: Leave me alone, can't you?

He grabs her again, a hand straying to her bottom.

LUBIN: Look, Claudine...

CLAUDINE: Help! Rape!

In alarm, LUBIN lets her go.

LUBIN: You're too hard on me. You shouldn't be so gorgeous if you don't want men feeling you up. Give us a kiss, at least.

CLAUDINE: All right, then – on the nose.

He offers his nose; she bites it.

LUBIN: Owww! You bitch!

CLAUDINE: That'll teach you to get fresh.

LUBIN: All I want's a bit of fun. Couldn't you just...?

CLAUDINE: You'll have to wait till we're married.

LUBIN: Just one kiss – on account, so to speak.

CLAUDINE: Nothing doing.

LUBIN: Please...

CLAUDINE: I've been tricked that way before. Go and tell the Vicomte I'm delivering his letter. Goodbye.

LUBIN: You've got a heart of stone, you have.

CLAUDINE: Charming!

LUBIN goes.

CLAUDINE: I'll give this to my mistress. But here she comes with her husband. I'll wait till she's alone. (*Waits to one side, unseen.*)

Enter DANDIN and ANGELIQUE.

GEORGE DANDIN: Oh, no – I'm not so easily deceived. I'm absolutely convinced that what I was told is true. I wasn't fooled by your antics this morning.

Enter CLITANDRE.

CLITANDRE: Ah! There she is! But she's got her husband with her.

GEORGE DANDIN: I could see it was true, in spite of all those faces you pulled. Have you no respect for me? I'm your husband, for Christ's sake. My God! Spare me your curtsies: that's not the sort of respect I'm talking about, so you needn't make fun of me.

ANGELIQUE: Make fun of you! I wouldn't dream of it.

GEORGE DANDIN: I know what you're thinking. I know... There you go again! I've had enough of this. You think I'm inferior to you, because you're a "lady of quality". Well, it's not me I want you to respect – it's the institution of marriage, which is sacred. Don't shrug your shoulders – as though I was talking nonsense.

ANGELIQUE: Who's shrugging their shoulders?

GEORGE DANDIN: You are! Jesus! I repeat: I'm your husband – you're supposed to respect me. Instead of which, you're treating me like dirt. It's just not good enough. I mean it. It's no use tossing your head and pouting.

ANGELIQUE: Me! I don't know what you mean.

GEORGE DANDIN: Well I do. I know your scornful ways. My blood may not be blue, but I come from a thoroughly respectable family. Why, we Dandins...

CLITANDRE: (*Behind ANGELIQUE, unseen by DANDIN.*) I must speak to you.

GEORGE DANDIN: What's that?

CLITANDRE kisses ANGELIQUE passionately, unseen by DANDIN.

ANGELIQUE: What's what? I didn't say anything.

CLITANDRE kisses ANGELIQUE again, and fondles her breasts.

GEORGE DANDIN: (*As CLITANDRE is going.*) There he is! The man who's sniffing round you.

ANGELIQUE: So? Is that my fault? What do you want me to do about it?

GEORGE DANDIN: What any wife would do, if she only wanted to please her husband. Say what you like, men don't pursue a woman unless she wants to be pursued. There's a certain mincing manner that attracts them, the way rotten meat attracts flies. Respectable wives have ways of scaring them off.

ANGELIQUE: Why would I want to do that? I'm not offended if men find me beautiful. On the contrary, it pleases me.

GEORGE DANDIN: And how am *I* supposed to take it, eh?

ANGELIQUE: Like an honest man who's glad to see his wife admired.

GEORGE DANDIN: That's crap! We Dandins aren't used to this sort of treatment.

ANGELIQUE: Tough. You may as well get this into your thick skull: I'm not about to bury myself alive with a husband. What? Must everything stop for a woman just because some man decides to marry her? Must we lose all contact with the living? Must we be dead to all pleasures and live only for our husbands? Why, that's sheer tyranny. I don't intend to die so young.

GEORGE DANDIN: So marriage is death, is it? Well, that's too bad: you're stuck with me.

ANGELIQUE: I wouldn't count on that, if I were you.

GEORGE DANDIN: Is this how you keep the vows you made me, in public?

ANGELIQUE

I didn't choose you, though. I had no say.
You never asked me for a "Yea" or "Nay".
My feelings simply didn't interest you.
No. It's my father that you're married to,
Since you consulted him, not me. What's more,
If you believe you've suffered wrongs, his door
Not mine's where you should lay them. As for me,
I never wanted you, nor can I see
Why I should be a slave to your demands.
With your permission, while I've got the chance,
I mean to use my youth – before it goes.
The pleasures I've been given to suppose
My age allows me: smart society
And lots of handsome men to flirt with me –
I want them and I'm having them, so there!
Don't even think of stopping me. Beware!
You've got a trying time ahead of you.
Just thank your stars I've nothing worse in view.

GEORGE DANDIN: So that's what you've got in mind, is it? Well, if you think I'm going to just sit there and take it, you're wrong.

ANGELIQUE: I'm quaking in my boots!

GEORGE DANDIN: I'd like to beat her face to a pulp. No one'd flirt with her then. Oof! I can't take any more of this. I'm off. (*Goes.*)

CLAUDINE: Madame, I could hardly wait for him to go: I have a message for you from you-know-who.

ANGELIQUE: Show me.

CLAUDINE hands her the letter, which she reads.

CLAUDINE: She seems pretty pleased with the contents.

ANGELIQUE: He certainly knows what to say! Courtiers have such style. Provincial men pale in comparison.

CLAUDINE: So the Dandins of this world aren't for you?

ANGELIQUE: Wait here and I'll give you my reply. (*Goes.*)

CLAUDINE: I don't think she needs me to tell her what to say. But here he comes again.

Enter CLITANDRE and LUBIN.

CLAUDINE: Well, monsieur, you've picked a first class messenger. (*Pointing disapprovingly at LUBIN.*)

CLITANDRE: I didn't dare send one of my servants. But, Claudine, I must reward you for all the trouble you've taken on my behalf.

CLAUDINE: No need for that, monsieur. I'm helping you because you deserve it, and because I like you.

CLITANDRE: (*Giving her some money.*) I'm obliged to you.

LUBIN: Give me that, since we're going to be married: I'll put it with mine.

CLAUDINE: I'll keep it for you, along with the kiss.

CLITANDRE: You gave your mistress my letter?

CLAUDINE: Yes. She's gone to write an answer.

CLITANDRE: But, Claudine, is there no way I can speak to her?

CLAUDINE: Yes. Come with me and I'll fix it.

CLITANDRE: But will she agree? Isn't it risky?

CLAUDINE: Oh, no: her husband's out. Besides, it's not him she has to worry about, it's her father. Get him on our side and the rest is easy.

CLITANDRE: I'm in your hands.

LUBIN: Well, I'll be...! What a clever wife I'm going to have! She's a bloody genius!

Exit CLAUDINE and CLITANDRE; enter DANDIN.

GEORGE DANDIN: There's that man again. If he'd just agree to tell her parents what he told me.

LUBIN: Ah! There you are, you blabbermouth! You promised me you'd keep quiet.

GEORGE DANDIN: I did?

LUBIN: Yes. You went and spilled the beans. Thanks to you the husband threw a full-scale wobbly. But I've learned my lesson: I won't tell you anything in future.

GEORGE DANDIN: Listen, friend.

LUBIN: If you hadn't gone and shot your mouth off, I'd have told you what's going on right now.

GEORGE DANDIN: What do you mean? What is going on?

LUBIN: Nothing. My lips are sealed. That's what you get for talking. You'll just have to lump it. (*Going.*)

GEORGE DANDIN: Wait a minute...

LUBIN: Sorry.

GEORGE DANDIN: I just want a word.

LUBIN: Nothing doing. You want to worm it out of me, don't you?

GEORGE DANDIN: Worm what out of you?

LUBIN: You can't fool me.

GEORGE DANDIN: It's not that. Listen.

LUBIN: Give up.

GEORGE DANDIN: Please.

LUBIN: Uh-uh.

GEORGE DANDIN: I'll give you...

LUBIN: I'm not interested. (*Goes.*)

GEORGE DANDIN

That fellow's clearly not the brainless twit
I took him for.

*He hears ANGELIQUE giggling in the house, goes to the keyhole
and looks through it.*

My God! That settles it!
He's with her now! Well, here's my chance to show
Her father what she's up to. How to, though?
If I go in, I'll scare the bastard off,
And just my word for it won't be enough –
Not for that pompous fart: he'll only say
I'm dreaming. Go and look for him? No way!
Knowing my luck, before I've found him, *he'll*

Gesturing at door to indicate CLITANDRE.

Have disappeared. But here's de Sotenville!

Enter M. DE SOTENVILLE.

GEORGE DANDIN: So, you wouldn't believe me before,
and your daughter got the better of me. But now I can
show you how she's treating me. Yes, thank God: my
disgrace is so obvious now, you can't doubt it any
longer.

M. DE SOTENVILLE: What, son-in-law? Still harping on
the same theme?

GEORGE DANDIN: Yes, I am. And with more reason than
ever.

M. DE SOTENVILLE: If you carry on like this, I shall go
mad.

GEORGE DANDIN: *You'll* go mad!

M. DE SOTENVILLE: Will you never tire of being a nuisance?

GEORGE DANDIN: No. But I'm tired of being taken for a fool.

M. DE SOTENVILLE: When will you rid yourself of these delusions?

GEORGE DANDIN: Not till I've rid myself of a wife who's disgracing me.

M. DE SOTENVILLE: Good God, son-in-law! What are you saying? I'll thank you not to be so offensive.

GEORGE DANDIN: Why the Hell shouldn't I be? Put yourself in my shoes.

M. DE SOTENVILLE: Don't forget, you have married a lady.

GEORGE DANDIN: How could I? You won't let me.

M. DE SOTENVILLE: In that case, speak of her with more respect.

GEORGE DANDIN: I will, when she starts showing *me* some. What? Does being a lady give her the right to treat me however she likes, while I daren't breathe?

M. DE SOTENVILLE: What are you talking about? She denied knowing the man this morning. You saw for yourself.

GEORGE DANDIN: What if I told you he was with her now?

M. DE SOTENVILLE: With her?

GEORGE DANDIN: Yes: in my house.

M. DE SOTENVILLE: In your house?

GEORGE DANDIN: That's right.

M. DE SOTENVILLE: If that is so, I shall take your side against her. The honour of my family is dearer

to me than anything else. If what you say is true,
I shall disown her and leave her at your mercy.

GEORGE DANDIN: Just follow me, then.

M. DE SOTENVILLE: You had better be right. If this is a
repeat of this morning's performance...

GEORGE DANDIN: See for yourself: here they come.
Now tell me: am I right or am I right?

Enter ANGELIQUE, CLITANDRE and CLAUDINE.

ANGELIQUE: Goodbye. I'm afraid my husband may find
you here. I must be careful.

CLITANDRE: Then you must arrange for me to see you
tonight.

ANGELIQUE: I'll do my best.

GEORGE DANDIN: Let's creep up on them from behind.

CLAUDINE: Ah! Madame, we've had it! Look, there's your
father – and your husband's with him.

CLITANDRE: Damnation!

ANGELIQUE: Act normal and leave this to me.
(*To CLITANDRE.*)

You have the nerve to try it on again,
After what happened earlier? Jesus! Men!
I've never seen such inconsistency:
First I'm informed that you're in love with me
And want to speak to me. I tell you straight,
In front of everyone: "Forget it, mate!"
Then you deny the whole thing. You protest
You meant me no offence. What happens next?
You have the utter cheek to call on me
And try to flirt with me – quite brazenly –
Uttering amorous absurdities
As though I might deceive my husband. Please!

Just what in God's name do you take me for?
A decent, well-bred woman, or a whore?
My parents inculcated into me
A sense of modesty and decency.
It's quite outrageous! If my father got
To hear of this, he'd show you what was what.
I'm too respectable to make a scene.
However, woman though I am, I mean
To show you I can settle my own scores:
I'll make you rue this insolence of yours.
And since you're not a gentleman, monsieur,
I won't be treating you as though you were.

CLAUDINE: (*To CLITANDRE.*) See who you're dealing with?

ANGELIQUE: Ah! Father! I didn't see you.

M. DE SOTENVILLE: My child, you have shown yourself a true de Sotenville, in modesty and in courage. Come here: let me embrace you. Son-in-law, you must be delighted. This whole episode must give you nothing but joy. I can understand your alarm, but happily your suspicions have been dispelled.

CLAUDINE: Too right. That's quite a wife you've got – you don't deserve her. You ought to kiss the ground she walks on.

GEORGE DANDIN: You treacherous little...!

M. DE SOTENVILLE: (*To DANDIN.*) What is it? Why do you not thank your wife for the love she has shown you?

ANGELIQUE: No, father, no. That won't be necessary. He doesn't owe me anything. What I did just then I did for myself, not him.

M. DE SOTENVILLE: Where are you going?

ANGELIQUE: In. I don't want to have to listen to his grovelling.

CLAUDINE: She's every reason to be angry. She deserves to be adored, and you treat her like dirt.

GEORGE DANDIN: You scheming little...

M. DE SOTENVILLE: She's still a bit upset about this morning. Give her a kiss and it will pass. Goodbye, son-in-law. As you see, you need not trouble yourself any more. Go in the pair of you and make peace. (*To DANDIN.*) You shouldn't have lost your temper: make it up to her; apologise. You must remember she has been strictly brought up: she is not used to being suspected of anything scandalous.

GEORGE DANDIN: Oh, isn't she?

Exeunt CLITANDRE, ANGELIQUE, CLAUDINE and M. DE SOTENVILLE.

GEORGE DANDIN

My nose is well and truly out of joint!
I don't say anything – well, what's the point?
Whoever had to suffer such disgrace?
Most men would opt for murder in my place.
But how about my wife? What subtlety!
You saw the way she put the blame on me
And looked the very soul of innocence.
With us, though, that's how every quarrel ends.
I ask you, will it always be this way?
Will I be grovelling till my dying day
To this, this harpy? Must I spend my life
Being humiliated by my wife?
Constantly thwarted by the way things look?
Balked of all hope of bringing her to book?
Oh, Heaven, take my part and help me show
The world what I've been forced to undergo.

ACT THREE

CLITANDRE, LUBIN.

CLITANDRE: It's almost midnight. I'm afraid we may be too late. Lubin! Damn it! I can't see where I'm going.

LUBIN: Monsieur? Where are you?

CLITANDRE: Here. Is this the way?

LUBIN: I think so. Christ! Is it dark, or what? No moon. What a night for it!

CLITANDRE: We can't see, but at least we can't be seen.

LUBIN: You're right. Tell me something, monsieur – you're a knowledgeable sort of bloke – why is it never day when it's night?

CLITANDRE: That's a big question. I haven't time to answer it just now. As I understand it, it has a lot to do with astronomical phenomena – the phases of the moon, that sort of thing. You've an inquiring mind, Lubin, I'll say that for you.

LUBIN: Thank you, monsieur. You know, I really think if I'd studied, I'd have thought of things no one's ever thought of before.

CLITANDRE: I don't doubt that for a moment. I can see you're a perceptive, intelligent fellow.

LUBIN: Too right, monsieur. You know, I understand Latin, even though I've never been taught it. The other day I saw * "ARS GRATIA ARTIS" written somewhere, and I knew at once what it meant.

CLITANDRE: Admirable! You can read, then?

LUBIN: Of course I can – but only capitals.

* NB: In Latin, "ars" is pronounced "arse"!

CLITANDRE: I think this must be the house. Claudine told me to whistle. (*He whistles.*)

LUBIN: God, what a miracle that Claudine is! She's worth her weight in gold. I don't mind admitting, I'm completely crazy about her.

CLITANDRE: Get a hold of yourself. There's work to be done. Your job's to talk to her.

LUBIN: Monsieur, I...

CLITANDRE: Sshh! I heard something.

Enter ANGELIQUE and CLAUDINE.

ANGELIQUE: Claudine?

CLAUDINE: I'm here, madame.

ANGELIQUE: Leave the door ajar.

CLAUDINE: All right. (*Does so.*)

CLITANDRE: It's them. Pssst!

ANGELIQUE: Pssst!

LUBIN: Pssst!

CLAUDINE: Pssst!

CLITANDRE: (*To CLAUDINE.*) Madame.

ANGELIQUE: (*To LUBIN.*) Yes?

LUBIN: (*To ANGELIQUE.*) Claudine.

CLAUDINE: (*To CLITANDRE.*) What is it?

CLITANDRE: (*To CLAUDINE.*) Ah! Madame, what joy!

LUBIN: (*To ANGELIQUE.*) Claudine, my love!

The two couples embrace and some fairly heavy-duty groping takes place. Then they all realise their mistake and exclaim.

CLAUDINE: (*To CLITANDRE, as he embraces her.*) Steady on, monsieur!

ANGELIQUE: (*As LUBIN embraces her.*) Lubin! What on earth do you think you're doing?

CLITANDRE: It's you, Claudine!

CLAUDINE: It is; don't stop, though; that was really nice.

LUBIN: It's you, madame! Can't see your own nose on a night like this.

ANGELIQUE: Quite so. Clitandre...?

CLITANDRE: Madame?

ANGELIQUE: My husband's snoring away upstairs.

CLITANDRE: He is? Excellent. Let's find a spot where we can sit and talk.

CLAUDINE: Good idea.

CLAUDINE, ANGELIQUE and CLITANDRE go and sit at the rear of the stage.

LUBIN: Claudine? Where are you?

Enter DANDIN.

GEORGE DANDIN: I know my wife's out here somewhere. These days, you see, I sleep with one eye open. I've got a shrewd idea what she's doing, too. Where is she?

LUBIN: Claudine? Claudine? Where the Hell are you? (*Mistaking DANDIN for CLAUDINE.*) Ah! There you are. What a brilliant trick we've played on that ponce of a master of yours! Your mistress says he's snoring away upstairs. He doesn't know that she and the Vicomte are together. I'd love to know what he's dreaming about. It's ridiculous! What business has he to be jealous of his wife, and want her to belong to him and no one else?

Did I say ridiculous? It's outrageous! The Vicomte's doing him a great honour. Claudine? Why don't you say something? Come on, let's find them – and give me that pretty little hand of yours – I want to kiss it. Ah! How sweet it is! Like eating sugar plums. (*He kisses DANDIN's hand; DANDIN pushes him away with a hand on his face.*) Hey! What do you think you're doing you... (*Realising his mistake.*)... oh, dear!

GEORGE DANDIN: Who the Hell are you? (*Hits LUBIN.*)

LUBIN: No one. (*Aside.*) If it's going to get rough, I'm off. (*Runs off to join the others.*)

GEORGE DANDIN: He's gone. So, my wife's at it again. I must send for her father at once: this means divorce. (*Calls into the house.*) Hello? Colin? Colin?

COLIN: (*Appearing at the window.*) Monsieur?

GEORGE DANDIN: Come here. And be quick about it.

COLIN: (*Jumps through the window.*) Here I am! You can't be much quicker than that.

GEORGE DANDIN: Where are you?

COLIN: Here, monsieur.

DANDIN goes to one side of the stage to speak to COLIN while COLIN goes to the other side to speak to him.

GEORGE DANDIN: We must keep our voices down. Listen: you're to go to my father-in-law's house and tell him I need him here right away. Make sure he realises it's urgent. Do you understand? Colin? Colin?

COLIN: (*From the other side of the stage.*) Monsieur?

GEORGE DANDIN: Where the Devil are you?

COLIN: Here.

They look for each other and cross over, each to the other's previous position.

GEORGE DANDIN: Christ, what a cretin! Where's he got to now? I said: go and fetch my father-in-law. Is that clear? He's to get over here at once. It's extremely important. Make damned sure that he realises that. All right? Colin? Answer me, for the love of God!

COLIN: (*From the other side of the stage.*) Monsieur?

GEORGE DANDIN: I've never seen such imbecility! He'll drive me mad! Come here!

They bump into one another.

GEORGE DANDIN: Silly sod! You damn near crippled me! Where *are* you? Come here! I want to give you a good thrashing. God knows, you've asked for it. (*To audience.*) I think he's trying to get away from me.

COLIN: (*To audience.*) Too right I am!

GEORGE DANDIN: Come here this minute!

COLIN: Not on your life!

GEORGE DANDIN: I'm warning you...

COLIN: No way, monsieur: you're going to belt me one.

GEORGE DANDIN: I won't lay a finger on you. I give you my word.

COLIN: Honest?

GEORGE DANDIN: Honest. Now, for the last time: COME HERE. Good. You're lucky I've got an errand for you. Otherwise I... well, some other time. Now, I'll say this just once more: you're to run and fetch my father-in-law. He's to come without delay. I don't care what he's doing. He's not to even bother getting dressed. This is a matter of life and death. Is that clear?

COLIN: Yes, monsieur. I think so.

GEORGE DANDIN: Off you go, then. And I want you back here as soon as possible.

COLIN goes.

GEORGE DANDIN: What a moron! I'm going in now, to wait for... But someone's coming. I'll bet it's my wife and... It's incredibly dark out here. She'll never see me. I'll listen in.

ANGELIQUE, CLITANDRE and CLAUDINE come back downstage.

ANGELIQUE: Goodbye. I must go in.

CLITANDRE: So soon?

ANGELIQUE: We've talked enough – well, for tonight, at least.

CLITANDRE: Ah, madame! How could I find the words I need in so short a time? It would take days to tell you how I feel.

ANGELIQUE: I'll hear more another time.

CLITANDRE: It's torture to me when you talk of parting. What torments I'll be suffering when you're gone. Was any man more miserable than I?

ANGELIQUE: I know we'll find a way to meet again.

CLITANDRE: Yes. But how can I forget that, when you leave me, you'll be going back to your husband? That he'll be tasting the delights I long for. That thought kills me. A husband's privileges are appalling to a lover.

ANGELIQUE: How can you possibly worry about that? Privileges indeed! What privileges? Do you think I could love a husband like him? Do you think I'd let him lay a finger on me? I married him because I had no choice. Because my father thinks of only one thing:

money. But I know how to get even with him. It would be absurd to show him more respect than he deserves. As for his so-called "conjugal rights", he's had them, I admit – but a long time ago now. Having had them and lost them: that's the deepest cut.

GEORGE DANDIN: (*Aside.*) That's wives for you: sluts, the lot of them. What I'm going to do to her when I get her alone... well, it doesn't bear thinking about. Her own father won't recognise her when I'm finished with her.

CLITANDRE: He certainly doesn't deserve you. A fiend like him married to an angel like you – sharing your bed – it's ridiculous. No, it's worse than ridiculous – it's disgusting.

GEORGE DANDIN: (*Aside.*) See how we husbands are treated? Poor wretches! Why do we let ourselves in for this sort of humiliation?

CLITANDRE: You deserve a better fate. You weren't made to be a peasant's wife.

GEORGE DANDIN: Would to God she was yours! You'd soon change your tune. I've had enough of this – I'm going in.

He goes in and locks and bolts the door.

CLAUDINE: Madame, if you want to slag your husband off any more you'd better hurry. Time's marching on.

CLITANDRE: Ah, Claudine! You're heartless!

ANGELIQUE: She's right, Clitandre. Let's go our separate ways.

CLITANDRE: Well, I suppose we must, since you insist. Think of me, at least. Think of the torment I'll be going through.

ANGELIQUE: Goodbye.

They embrace passionately.

LUBIN: Claudine, my love? Where are you? I want to say goodnight.

CLAUDINE: Consider it said. Now, off you go.

Exit CLITANDRE and LUBIN.

ANGELIQUE: Let's go in – quietly.

CLAUDINE: We can't. The door's locked. We're trapped!

ANGELIQUE: There's no cause for alarm. I've got the master key.

CLAUDINE: Thank God for that! Open it, then – gently.

ANGELIQUE: Damn! It's bolted! What are we going to do?

CLAUDINE: Call Colin.

ANGELIQUE: Colin, Colin, Colin.

GEORGE DANDIN: (*Putting his head out of the window.*) Colin, Colin? I've caught you out, madame. So, you go on escapades while I'm asleep. Well, I'm glad – and glad to see you out there at this hour.

ANGELIQUE: Oh? And what's so terrible about taking the night air?

GEORGE DANDIN: The night air! Don't make me laugh! I know what you've been up to, you whore. I know all about your rendez-vous. I heard you billing and cooing. I heard you singing my praises. But I'm about to get my own back at last. Your father's going to have to believe me this time. I've sent for him. He'll be here any moment now.

ANGELIQUE: Oh, God!

CLAUDINE: Madame...?

GEORGE DANDIN

No wonder you're aghast.
This is my hour of triumph. Yes, at last
I've found a way to stop your carrying on.
So far you've made me look a simpleton –
Managed to con your father, God knows how,
And look like innocence itself. Not now.
Till now, no matter what I did or said
You always seemed to be a step ahead,
But this time I'm afraid you've gone too far –
You're going to be exposed for what you are.

ANGELIQUE: Let me in. Please!

GEORGE DANDIN: Ohhh, no. We're waiting for your
father. I want him to find you out in the street in the small
hours. Meanwhile you can rack your brains for some new
excuse to get you out of this mess. Perhaps you were on a
nocturnal pilgrimage; or visiting a friend in labour.

ANGELIQUE: No. What's the use of defending myself
when you know the truth? I'm not going to hide
anything from you.

GEORGE DANDIN: That's because you're cornered.

ANGELIQUE: I'm in the wrong. I admit it. But I beg of
you, don't expose me to my father's anger. Let me in.
Before it's too late.

GOERGE DANDIN: Forget it.

ANGELIQUE: Please, my love. I'll do anything to make it
up to you. And I mean: anything...

GEORGE DANDIN: "My love"! I'm your love now you
know you're trapped.

ANGELIQUE: Look, I promise you I'll behave in future. I won't...

GEORGE DANDIN: It's no use, Angélique. You've pushed me to the limit and beyond. I'm not losing this round. I'm determined to expose you. I want to see your father's face when I tell him what his precious daughter's been up to. I don't think we'll be hearing so much about the "honour of the de Sotenvilles" after that.

ANGELIQUE: For pity's sake, listen to me.

GEORGE DANDIN: Go on, then.

ANGELIQUE

You've ample cause to feel aggrieved, it's true,
Given the shameful way I've treated you:
Yes, I went out while you were sound asleep,
And yes, I had a rendez-vous to keep
With the man that you'd suspected all along.
But then, was what I did so very wrong?
What do I know about the world? I'm young –
I'd found a handsome man to flirt with me –
I haven't lived – I simply didn't see
How dangerous his sort of thing can be.

GEORGE DANDIN: A likely story!

ANGELIQUE

                No excuses, though:
I've acted quite despicably, I know.
I want you to forgive and to forget,
That's all. I'll be forever in your debt
If you can bring yourself to pity me
And spare me the disgrace, the agony
Of being hounded by my father. Yes,
I promise you, a little tenderness
Will kindle feelings here (*Hand on heart.*) to which the ties
Of marriage never could have given rise –

Still less my father's power. I promise you,
There'll never be another rendez-vous –
No more admirers – you're the only one
I'm ever going to look at from now on.
You have my word: from this day forth I'll be
The perfect pattern of fidelity.
The true, the tender love you've given me
Throughout our marriage, which, until today,
I've done – well – precious little to repay,
Will be returned at last: I've learned from you –
I'm going to change now – I'm determined to.

GEORGE DANDIN: Hypocrite! You're not going to
deceive me. Not this time. You want to destroy me. Well,
I won't let you. The boot's on the other foot, and that's
where it's going to stay. If I weaken – if I let you off –
and God help me, there's a part of me that wants to do
just that – then you'd be at it again next week. On and
on it'd go, till I was in an early grave.

ANGELIQUE: That's not true. Just do this one thing for me...

GEORGE DANDIN: Enough. I'm adamant.

ANGELIQUE: Show some pity.

GEORGE DANDIN: No.

ANGELIQUE: Please!!

GEORGE DANDIN: It's no use.

ANGELIQUE: For the love of God...

GEORGE DANDIN: No, no and thrice no. I want your
father to know the truth about you. I want to see you
squirm. Damn it, if the only way to tame you is to
humiliate you, then that's what I'm going to do.

ANGELIQUE: Very well then, if you're bent on disgracing
me. But I warn you, a desperate woman is capable of
anything. I'm going to make you well and truly sorry.

GEORGE DANDIN: Oh? How?

ANGELIQUE: I'm going to kill myself – with this knife.

GEORGE DANDIN: Go ahead! See if I care.

ANGELIQUE

                  Oh, you'll care:
Aren't all and sundry only too aware
Of how we quarrel? How you've hated me
Since we were married? There will only be
One explanation when they find me dead:
They'll heap their accusations on your head.
You've seen what sort of man my father is:
Whose sense of justice is as keen as his?
He'll take the bloodiest revenge the law –
Or, failing that, his wrongs – give warrant for.
What's more, I won't have been the only wife
Who took this course – who sacrificed her life,
While suffering unspeakable distress,
To make a husband rue his heartlessness.

GEORGE DANDIN: I'd think twice about this if I were you: suicide's out of date.

ANGELIQUE: I'll do it, I promise you. Unless you let me in, I'll show you what a woman's capable of when you push her to the limit.

GEORGE DANDIN: What a lot of rubbish! You're just trying to frighten me and I'm afraid it won't work. You see, I know better than anyone what a devious bitch you are.

ANGELIQUE

All right, you leave me no choice. Now you'll see
If I'm in earnest: this is going to be
A blessing for us both. Ah! I expire!
Oh, Heaven! Grant the vengeance I desire
And may the man who brought this death on me

Be justly punished for his cruelty!
The world knows what a fiend my husband is –
Let *him* be held responsible for this –
Pay with his life for my untimely death –
I curse George Dandin with my dying breath!   ·

GEORGE DANDIN: Eh? Can she really be so malicious
as to stab herself and hang me in the process? Where's
a candle? Let's take a look. God knows, she's capable
of anything to get back at me. Angélique? Angéli – i
– ique...? Don't die yet. I'm coming, my dearest.
Everything's going to be all right, you'll see. Just give
me a little time. I've seen the error of my ways, really
I have. Hello? Are you there? (*Pause.*) I do believe
she's done it. Oh, my God! What am I going to do?
She's right you know: I am to blame in a way. If I'd
treated her better – shown her a bit more love; a bit
more... attention – if you know what I mean – it might
never have come to this. Poor creature! I'll miss her.
What's going to become of me? I'm done for.

ANGELIQUE: (*To CLAUDINE.*) Pssst! (*In a whisper.*) Let's
each stand to one side of the door.

*They do so. DANDIN comes out holding a candle; he doesn't see them;
they go in and immediately lock the door.*

GEORGE DANDIN: I don't believe it! There's no one
here. Can you beat that? She could see she wasn't getting
anywhere so she's done a bunk, the little... So much the
better. Things'll look even worse now. What's this? The
door's locked itself. Hello! Anyone! Let me in at once!

ANGELIQUE: (*Appearing at the window with CLAUDINE.*)
What? Oh, it's you. Where have you been, you bastard?
What time is this to be coming home? It's almost light. Is
this any way for a respectable husband to be carrying on?

CLAUDINE: Too right! Gallivanting the night away and
leaving your young wife alone in the house, poor girl!

Mind you, she's better off with you out than in, considering the way you treat her, you vicious bastard!

GEORGE DANDIN: That's it, Claudine. Consider yourself dismissed.

CLAUDINE: Oh, yes? You know you'd never have the guts to throw me out.

GEORGE DANDIN: I haven't time to discuss this now. Angélique, do you seriously expect me to believe you were inside all the time? You can't have been. It's obviously a pack of lies.

ANGELIQUE: To Hell with you! I'm sick of your tantrums. I'm going to tell my father what you've done.

GEORGE DANDIN: How dare you talk to me like that, you wh...ell*oooo*, monsieur de Sotenville!

This as M. DE SOTENVILLE enters in his nightclothes, carrying a lantern.

ANGELIQUE: Come here, father. I want you to punish my husband for his insolence. His wits are so addled by wine. He no longer knows what he's saying or doing. He's sent for you himself to witness his outrageous behaviour. He's kept me waiting outside all night, and he's about to tell you *he* has a grievance against *me*; that I left his bed on an "escapade", if you please, while he was asleep; and I don't know what nonsense besides. Well, you're not to believe him. He's insane. And I don't mean that metaphorically, either.

GEORGE DANDIN: Damn her eyes!

CLAUDINE: He keeps saying he was at home and we were out. We can't get the idea out of his head. My mistress is right, monsieur: he's mad. I've said it before and I'll say it again: he should have been locked up years ago.

M. DE SOTENVILLE: (*To DANDIN.*) What is the meaning of this, son-in-law? How dare you send for me at this late hour?

GEORGE DANDIN: I...

ANGELIQUE: It's no use, father: I can't possibly be expected to tolerate a husband like him. I've reached the end of my tether. What he's just said to me – it's too hurtful.

M. DE SOTENVILLE: (*To DANDIN.*) By God, you're a swine!

CLAUDINE: I can't bear to see her treated this way. Poor thing! Something has to be done, monsieur. It's got to stop – really it has.

GEORGE DANDIN: Might I just...?

M. DE SOTENVILLE: No you might not – you ought to die of shame.

GEORGE DANDIN: If you'd let me get a word in...

ANGELIQUE: You've only got to listen to him and you'll see we're right about his state of mind. He'll tell you all sorts of rubbish.

GEORGE DANDIN: If I could...

CLAUDINE: (*To M. DE SOTENVILLE.*) I wouldn't go near him if I were you. He's not just off his tree – he's drunk as well. In fact he's drunk so much I can smell him from here. Don't get too close.

GEORGE DANDIN: Monsieur de...

M. DE SOTENVILLE: Keep away! You reek of wine. Don't try anything, either. Don't forget, I come from a family of warriors. Why, there was a baron de Sotenville who...

GEORGE DANDIN: For pity's sake...

M. DE SOTENVILLE: Keep away, I tell you!

GEORGE DANDIN: (*Suddenly enraged.*) Keep away! KEEP AWAY! I'm sick to death of this! I've had enough of being trampled all over by you lot. I'm going to have my say if it's the last thing I... AH!

DANDIN clutches his chest, doubles up in agony and collapses. Overcoming his qualms, M. DE SOTENVILLE bends over him and loosens his clothes. At first it seems all's up with him, but then he comes round.

M. DE SOTENVILLE: I say, Dandin! Are you all right?

GEORGE DANDIN: Just about. What happened?

M. DE SOTENVILLE: (*To DANDIN.*) You had me worried for a minute there.

CLAUDINE: It would have served him damned well right if he'd breathed his last then and there. What did you have to go and save him for?

GEORGE DANDIN: (*To M. DE SOTENVILLE.*) Listen... monsieur, I swear to you, I haven't left the house. It was Angélique that went out.

ANGELIQUE: What did I tell you just now? The ravings of a man whose lost his wits.

CLAUDINE: She's right, monsieur.

M. DE SOTENVILLE: (*To DANDIN.*) I think you must be making fun of me. (*To ANGELIQUE.*) Angélique, come out here.

GEORGE DANDIN: I swear to God I was in the house. It was...

M. DE SOTENVILLE: Silence! I'm tired of your ravings. Besides, if you go on like this we'll have a corpse on our hands.

GEORGE DANDIN: May lightning strike me if...

M. DE SOTENVILLE: CALM DOWN, can't you!! You must apologise to your wife.

GEORGE DANDIN: Me apologise to...?

M. DE SOTENVILLE: Yes. At once.

GEORGE DANDIN: But...

M. DE SOTENVILLE: DON'T ANSWER ME BACK!! I'll teach you to fool about with a man of my standing.

GEORGE DANDIN: Ah! George Dandin! George Dandin!

ANGELIQUE comes out of the house.

M. DE SOTENVILLE: Come, Angélique. Dandin must ask your forgiveness.

ANGELIQUE: Forgiveness! How can I possibly forgive him, after what he's said and done to me? No, father, it's out of the question. I want a separation. I can't live with him a moment longer.

CLAUDINE: You must agree to it, monsieur. Can't you see she's desperate?

M. DE SOTENVILLE: My child, a separation would inevitably involve a tremendous scandal. You must set your husband an example and be patient.

ANGELIQUE: Impossible, I'm afraid. I can't be patient after what he's put me through.

M. DE SOTENVILLE: You must. (*Beat; solemn.*) I order you to.

ANGELIQUE: That's different. I'll say no more. Your power over me is absolute.

CLAUDINE: The girl's a wonder! What submissiveness! I still believe you're making a mistake.

M. DE SOTENVILLE: When I want your opinion, Claudine, I shall ask for it. You're a servant: you should speak only when you're spoken too – if then.

ANGELIQUE: It's galling to have to forget such injuries, but no matter how he treats me I must obey you.

CLAUDINE: Ahhhhh!!

M. DE SOTENVILLE: That's the spirit! Come here, Angélique. Let's have a go at reconciliation. If it doesn't work out – and the accounts look a little better next year – well, maybe we shall have to think again.

ANGELIQUE: This won't do any good, you know. It'll be the same story in no time. Tomorrow morning, in fact, if past form is anything to go by. Isn't that so... husband? This is the pattern of things to come.

M. DE SOTENVILLE: Oh, no it isn't – not if I can help it. (*To DANDIN.*) Now, on your knees.

GEORGE DANDIN: On my knees? Again!

M. DE SOTENVILLE: Yes. And be quick about it.

GEORGE DANDIN: (*Kneeling.*) Oh, God! What must I say?

M. DE SOTENVILLE: "Madame, I beg you to forgive my folly."

GEORGE DANDIN: Madame, I beg you to forgive my folly. (*Aside.*) In marrying you.

M. DE SOTENVILLE: "And I promise to behave better in future."

GEORGE DANDIN: And I promise to behave better in future.

M. DE SOTENVILLE: Good. And mind you do. I won't tolerate any more of your impertinence. If there's any repetition of today's performance, I shall have to teach

you the respect due to your wife and her family. But it's
almost dawn. Go in, and try to learn some moderation.
(*Goes, followed by ANGELIQUE and CLAUDINE.*)

GEORGE DANDIN:

I give up: I can see no remedy.
No, when you're married to a slut, like me,
There's just one course of action you can take –
That's throw yourself into the nearest lake,
Not that I'd ever have the courage to.
I bid you all a bilious adieu.

THE END.

SCAPIN

translated by Ranjit Bolt

Characters

OCTAVE,
Argante's son, in love with Hyacinte

SILVESTRE,
Argante's servant

SCAPIN,
Géronte's servant

HYACINTE,
in love with Octave

ARGANTE,
a rich merchant

GERONTE,
another rich merchant

LEANDRE,
Géronte's son, in love with Zerbinetta

CARLE,
a servant

ZERBINETTA,
in love with Léandre

NERINE,
Zerbinetta's nurse

ACT ONE

OCTAVE, SILVESTRE.

OCTAVE: Shit! Are you sure?

SILVESTRE: Yes, sir. Your father's back, all right.

OCTAVE: His ship put in this morning?

SILVESTRE: That's right, sir.

OCTAVE: And he's found a wife for me?

SILVESTRE: Yes, sir.

OCTAVE: Old *Géronte's* daughter?

SILVESTRE: Old *Géronte's* daughter.

OCTAVE: That's why she was sent here from Tarentum?

SILVESTRE: Yes, sir.

OCTAVE: My uncle told you?

SILVESTRE: Your uncle told me.

OCTAVE: My father wrote to him about it?

SILVESTRE: Yes, sir.

OCTAVE: And *he's* been keeping an eye on us?

SILVESTRE: Your uncle, sir. Yes, sir.

OCTAVE: Oh for god's sake, do I have to squeeze every word out of you? Tell me the whole story.

SILVESTRE: That *is* the whole story.

OCTAVE: It's a catastrophe. What am I going to do?

SILVESTRE: Don't ask *me.* I'm as flummoxed as you.

OCTAVE: I'm up shit creek without a paddle.

SILVESTRE: *I'm* up shit creek without a *boat.*

OCTAVE: He'll crucify me when he finds out.

SILVESTRE: He'll beat me black and blue.

OCTAVE: How the Hell do I get out of this mess?

SILVESTRE: You should have thought of that before you got into it.

OCTAVE: Oh, belt up! It's no use being wise after the event.

SILVESTRE: You've been such a bloody idiot, though.

OCTAVE: What in God's name am I going to *do*?

Enter SCAPIN.

SCAPIN: What's wrong, monsieur Octave? You seem in a bit of a pother.

OCTAVE: Oh, Scapin, my goose is cooked. To a frazzle. I'm the wretchedest man on earth. Ohhhhhh... fuck!

SCAPIN: Hmmm. How come?

OCTAVE: You don't know?

SCAPIN: Nope.

OCTAVE: My father's in town. With old Géronte. They've gone and got a bloody bride for me.

SCAPIN: So? What's the problem?

OCTAVE: Don't you realise why I'm so upset?

SCAPIN: No. But you're about to tell me. And then I can help you out. I'll smooth the course of true love if I can.

OCTAVE: Ah! Scapin. If you could just think of something, anything, to get me out of this hole, this *abyss*. I'd be eternally in your debt.

SCAPIN: To tell you the truth, I can pull just about anything off if I put my mind to it. It's a god-given talent. I'm a genius, I am. A master of skull-duggery. At any rate, that's what the ignorant masses like to call it. Tricks might be a better word. Or ruses. No, let's say... elegant flights of ingenuity. I think I can claim, with all due modesty, that for stratagems and intrigues there's scarcely ever been a cannier man. Yes, I'll almost certainly go down in history. I'm a phenomenon. A miracle-worker. Of course, no one ever gets their just deserts in this day and age. I've given the whole business up. I had no choice after the last scrape I got into.

OCTAVE: A scrape? What sort of scrape?

SCAPIN: A brush with the law, monsieur. A bloody enormous brush.

OCTAVE: The law, eh?

SCAPIN: Yeees. We didn't quite see eye to eye on something.

OCTAVE: You and the law.

SCAPIN: Me and the law. I was hard done by, I was. I got so disillusioned with the age in which we live that I decided to retire. But what the Hell, let's hear the problem anyway.

OCTAVE: Well, Scapin, as you know, two months ago Géronte and my father went off on a journey. A business trip it was. Some sort of joint venture.

SCAPIN: That's right, yes.

OCTAVE: And my father told Silvestre to keep an eye on me, and Géronte told *you* to keep an eye on Léandre.

SCAPIN: Yes, and I have.

OCTAVE: Then Léandre met a young gipsy girl and fell in love with her.

SCAPIN: So he did.

OCTAVE: And since we're such close friends he told me about it at once. I met the girl. She was pretty enough, but nothing like what he'd cracked her up to be. He was besotted. Obsessed. He talked about her all the bloody time. According to him she was a queen, a goddess: as beautiful as the day is long; incredibly intelligent; unbelievably charming; sharp; witty; the works... he'd even give me verbatim accounts of conversations he'd had with her. And when I wasn't bowled over he got angry. Said I was imperceptive. Insensitive. Didn't understand what a wonderful thing love was. Et cetera, et cetera.

SCAPIN: Riii-iiight, but where's all this leading?

OCTAVE: One day we went to pay a call on the girl's guardian. On the way we passed through a series of ramshackle backstreets, and in one of them we heard sobbing and moaning. It seemed to be coming from a shabby little house on the corner. We went to enquire, and the housekeeper told us, if we wanted to see a really heart-rending sight, we should come upstairs.

SCAPIN: Riii-iiight... I still don't see the point of all this.

OCTAVE: I was curious and I made Léandre go up with me to see what it was all about. The housekeeper showed us into a poky upstairs bedroom, where an old woman lay dying. There was a young woman with her who was weeping uncontrollably. She was astonishingly beautiful. As beautiful as it's possible to be.

SCAPIN: (*Playful scepticism.*) *Ohhhh* yes?

OCTAVE: (*Bristling.*) *Yes.* Anyone else would have looked terrible. I mean, she was weeping; she was wearing a miserable little shift and a tatty nightgown; she had a dirty linen cap on, tied back on top of her head; and her hair looked as though it hadn't been done in years; it was a total mess. But *she* still managed to look ravishing.

SCAPIN: I think I can guess what's coming next.

OCTAVE: Oh, Scapin, if you'd only seen her, you'd have been smitten too.

SCAPIN: I'm sure. In fact, I'm smitten as it is.

OCTAVE: Her grief was absolutely irresistible.

SCAPIN: Of course.

OCTAVE: The way she flung herself onto the dying woman. It certainly *was* heart-rending to see. "Mother!" she sobbed. "Oh, dearest, *dearest* mother!" What a sweet nature! What a captivating creature!

SCAPIN: All very touching, I'm sure. So you've fallen for her.

OCTAVE: Scapin, *anyone* would have fallen for her.

SCAPIN: Of course.

OCTAVE: Well, I tried to console her as best I could, and then we left. I asked Léandre what he thought of her. He replied, rather coldly, that she wasn't bad-looking. This annoyed me, and I decided not to tell him how I felt about her.

SILVESTRE: You'd better cut this story short, monsieur, or we'll be here till tomorrow. Allow me: (*To SCAPIN.*) he's smitten; he'll die if he doesn't see her again; but the housekeeper won't let him, she being the girl's guardian now the old woman's dead; he's in despair; he begs to be allowed to see her; he pleads; he bleats; he entreats; nothing doing. The girl may be penniless, and with no visible means of support, but she comes from a respectable family, and he can't see her, says the housekeeper, unless he agrees to marry her. By now he's more in love with her than ever; the difficulties have increased his passion; he weighs it up; he mulls it over; he hesitates; he meditates; he comes to a decision; he's been married for three days.

SCAPIN: I see.

SILVESTRE: Add to that the fact that his father's back, two months early; and that his uncle's found out about the marriage; and that his father wants him to marry Géronte's daughter, by his second wife, who he married twenty years ago in Tarentum...

OCTAVE:... *and* the fact that the girl's got no money, and I won't have any either now...

SCAPIN: Is that all? You're making a mountain out of a molehill. What's all the fuss about? I'll deal with those old gits. Leave this to me.

OCTAVE: Here she comes now – her name's Hyacinte, by the way.

HYACINTE: (*Entering.*) Ah! Octave. Is this true? You're father's back? He's found a wife for you?

OCTAVE: Yes, Hyacinte, my love, I'm afraid so. The news has killed me. But what's this? Tears, my darling? Please don't cry. You can't believe I've had a change of heart? Don't you realise how much I love you?

HYACINTE: Perhaps you do now, but will you always?

OCTAVE: How could anyone *stop* loving *you*?

HYACINTE: Men are different from women. They fall out of love as fast as they fall in.

OCTAVE: My dearest Hyacinte, I'm not like other men. I'll love you till the day I die.

HYACINTE: I want to believe you. I'm sure you mean what you say. But you're totally dependant on your father, who wants you to marry someone else. And if you did... oh god, Octave, I know it would destroy me.

OCTAVE: Dear Hyacinte, I'll leave Naples, I'll *die*, but I won't desert you. My father can go to Hell. I haven't seen this daughter of Géronte's. I don't know who she is. But I loathe her already. And I wish there were oceans between her and me. So don't cry. Please, my darling. It breaks my heart to see these tears.

HYACINTE: Well, I shall accept my fate.

OCTAVE: We must be brave. Fortune will favour us.

HYACINTE: It will, as long as you're true to me.

OCTAVE: I shall be. I swear.

HYACINTE: And I'll try not to cry.

SCAPIN: (*Aside.*) The girl seems quite bright. Not bad-looking either.

OCTAVE: (*Pointing to SCAPIN.*) This is our man. Scapin. He's going to help us.

SCAPIN: I said I'd retired, monsieur, but since you're begging me...

OCTAVE: Absolutely. Our ship's got caught in a storm and we're begging you to take the helm.

SCAPIN: (*To HYACINTE.*) And you, mademoiselle Hyacinte, what do *you* say?

HYACINTE: I can only echo Octave: please, monsieur Scapin, by all you hold most dear, steer our ship to shore; save our love.

SCAPIN: All right, it's not as if I've got a heart of stone – I'm at your service.

OCTAVE: And as far as...

SCAPIN: Not a word about money! (*To HYACINTE.*) You'd better go, mademoiselle. And don't you fret yourself: your ship is in safe hands. (*To OCTAVE.*) As for you, monsieur, you must bear up and grit your teeth. Your father'll be here any minute.

OCTAVE: (*Terrified.*) Oh my god!

SCAPIN: Now now. Stiff upper lip. He mustn't see any sign of weakness. He's bound to interrogate you.

OCTAVE: I'll try to keep cool.

SCAPIN: Tell you what, I'll rehearse you; take you through a mock interrogation. All right? Come on, then, chin up, jaw out, expression firm.

OCTAVE: Like this?

SCAPIN: Bit firmer.

OCTAVE: Like this?

SCAPIN: Not bad. Now then, I'm your father; I'm going to ask you some questions, and I want you to answer me just as though I was him. Here we go then: "Yoooouuuu *scoundrel* You *rooooooogue* You worthless, dishonest, treacherous lump of dogshit on the pavement of my life! What sort of son are you? How dare you show your face after what you've done, youuuuuu *swine* No sooner have I gone than you betray me! Is this how you repay my love and kindness, monster? Is this all the respect you have for me? Wretch! Renegade! Reprobate! You married secretly! Without my consent! How dare you?! *Answer* me, you ponce, you poppinjay! How *Daaaarrrre* you?!" Now, explain yourself. (*Silence.*) Well go on, say something!

OCTAVE: I can't. I'm petrified. That was so convincing!

SCAPIN: Give it a try.

OCTAVE: All right then, here goes. I'm going to be really firm now.

SCAPIN: You are?

OCTAVE: Yes.

SCAPIN: Good, coz here he comes.

OCTAVE: Oh, Christ! Oh Heaven help me! (*Running off.*)

SCAPIN: Hey! Don't run off! He's bottled out. What a wimp! *We'd* better talk to the old sod.

SILVESTRE: What'll we say?

SCAPIN: Leave it to me. Just back me up.

Enter ARGANTE.

ARGANTE: (*Who thinks he's alone.*) Who ever heard of such a thing? Outrageous!

SCAPIN: (*To SILVESTRE.*) He knows already, and he's so pissed off about it he's talking to himself.

ARGANTE: (*Still thinking he's alone.*) How dare he?!

SCAPIN: (*To SILVESTRE.*) Let's eavesdrop.

ARGANTE: I'd like to hear his explanation.

SCAPIN: (*Aside.*) Thought so.

ARGANTE: (*Still thinking he's alone.*) Will they try and deny it?

SCAPIN: (*Aside.*) Nope.

ARGANTE: (*Still thinks he's alone.*) Or excuse it?

SCAPIN: (*Aside.*) Maybe.

ARGANTE: (*Still thinks he's alone.*) They're bound to spin some sort of yarn.

SCAPIN: (*Aside.*) We might.

ARGANTE: (*Still thinks he's alone.*) Well it won't wash.

SCAPIN: (*Aside.*) We'll see about that.

ARGANTE: (*Still thinks he's alone.*) They're not putting one over on *me*.

SCAPIN: (*Aside.*) Don't be too sure.

ARGANTE: (*Still thinks he's alone.*) I'll find a safe place and lock the boy up.

SCAPIN: (*Aside.*) Oh, you will, will you?

ARGANTE: (*Still thinks he's alone.*) And as for that little turd, Silvestre, I'll thrash him to within an inch of his life.

SILVESTRE: (*To SCAPIN.*) Thought that was coming.

ARGANTE: (*Seeing SILVESTRE.*) Ah! Aha! There you are. The trusty guardian of youth!

SCAPIN: It's great to have you back with us, monsieur Argante.

ARGANTE: Hello, Scapin. (*To SILVESTRE.*) So this is how you carry out my instructions. My son seems to have behaved in an *exemplary* fashion during my absence. Well? What have you got to say for yourself.

SCAPIN: How are you, monsieur? All right?

ARGANTE: Yes, thank you. (*To SILVESTRE.*) You! Shitwit! Say something.

SCAPIN: Did you have a good journey?

ARGANTE: Wonderful, thank you. Now can I explode in peace, please?

SCAPIN: Explode?

ARGANTE: Yes.

SCAPIN: At who?

ARGANTE: This little twerp here.

SCAPIN: What for?

ARGANTE: Haven't you heard what's been going on?

SCAPIN: I heard something, yes. Nothing especially awful, though.

ARGANTE: Nothing especially awful! Nothing especially awful! What could be worse, I'd like to know?

SCAPIN: Weeelll, you could have a point.

ARGANTE: It was a preposterous thing to do.

SCAPIN: I suppose you're right.

ARGANTE: For a boy to marry without his father's consent?

SCAPIN: You've got a legitimate grouse. But I wouldn't make too much of a fuss if I were you.

ARGANTE: Balls! I'll make as much fuss as I bloody well like. Legitimate grouse? I've got a whole sodding covey of 'em!

SCAPIN: So you have, monsieur, so you have. I was angry myself when I heard about it. I took your part I did. Blew the boy up like nobody's business. Just you ask him how I blew him up. "Is this the respect you show your father?" I said. "Why, you're not fit to lick the ground he walks on." I got as furious as you. But what the Hell, I calmed down eventually. After all, it's not *such* a heinous crime, when all's said and done.

ARGANTE: Bullshit. Of course it's heinous. He's married a nobody. Just like that. Out of the blue.

SCAPIN: He had no choice. It was his destiny.

ARGANTE: Oh, excellent excuse!

SCAPIN: What I mean is, the boy was, how shall I put it?, committed – fatally.

ARGANTE: And how exactly did he manage that?

SCAPIN: You can't expect him to be as prudent as you. He's young. Boys will be boys. Look at my master, monsieur Léandre: I'm always going on at him, trying to keep him in line, and now he's done something even worse.

ARGANTE: Worse than Octave?

SCAPIN: Much worse. And what about you? Weren't you young once? Did you never go astray? Eh? I've heard stories, you know. They say you were quite a skirt-chaser in your day. One of the randiest lads of your generation. "I've started so I'll finish." That was your motto.

ARGANTE: I can't deny I had my share of fun. But it was always strictly bed. I never married any of them.

SCAPIN: But what's he supposed to do? He meets a girl. She takes a shine to him. (He gets that from you, of course: to see him is to love him.) He's smitten. He starts calling on her. He whispers a lot of nonsense in her ear, and sighs, and gets all passionate. She falls for it. He takes things a stage further. Then her family find out and force his hand and he ends up having to marry her.

SILVESTRE: (*Aside.*) He's good!

SCAPIN: Would you rather they'd killed him? Better married than dead.

ARGANTE: This isn't what I was told.

SCAPIN: (*Pointing to SILVESTRE.*) Ask him then.

ARGANTE: (*To SILVESTRE.*) *Was* he forced?

SILVESTRE: Yes, monsieur.

SCAPIN: Would I lie to you?

ARGANTE: Then he has a case: he must go to a notary and get it annulled.

SCAPIN: He doesn't want to do that.

ARGANTE: He was *forced.* It's not a bona fide marriage.

SCAPIN: D'you want him to admit that he was afraid? That he let them push him into it? That's not his style. He'd be letting himself down – *and* you.

ARGANTE: Crap!

SCAPIN: It's a question of honour.

ARGANTE: Bilge.

SCAPIN: Well he won't do it.

ARGANTE: He sodding will.

SCAPIN: He bloody won't.

ARGANTE: I'll cut him off without a sou.

SCAPIN: You wouldn't.

ARGANTE: I would.

SCAPIN: You haven't the heart.

ARGANTE: I have.

SCAPIN: Fatherly feelings...

ARGANTE: Piffle.

SCAPIN: Blood is thicker than water.

ARGANTE: Poppycock.

SCAPIN: I know you. You're an old softy.

ARGANTE: Softy my arse. Now if you don't mind, this conversation is starting to raise my blood pressure. (*To SILVESTRE.*) Find that wretched son of mine. I'm off to break the news to Géronte. And Christ alone knows how I'm going to tell him. The disgrace! The humiliation! What a disaster!

SCAPIN: Monsieur, if *I* can be of any use, I'm at your service.

ARGANTE: (*Sarcasm.*) Oh, Scapin, that is *wonderful* to know. (*Aside, going.*) Why did I lose my daughter? I could have made *her* my heir. Why did he have to be my only son. I wish to god I had another one!

SILVESTRE: I thought you handled that pretty well. But what about money? We're in dire financial straights, you know. Hounded by creditors on all sides.

SCAPIN: Leave it to me. All we need's a man we can trust, to act out a particular part. Now hang on, just cock your hat a bit and stick one leg out like so. Hand on hip like so. Swagger, you know. And try and look terrifying. Now strut about a bit. Not bad. Come with me. I've got some tricks for disguising your face and your voice.

SILVESTRE: No brushes with the law please.

SCAPIN: Come along. We're comrades now. One for both and both for one. We might get a year or two in the galleys, but what the Hell, we can take it.

End of Act One.

ACT TWO

GERONTE, ARGANTE.

GERONTE: They should be here today. A sailor who'd just got here from Tarentum told me he'd seen my man about to embark. Things don't look hopeful for my daughter though. She might as well have stayed put. Your son seems to have dropped a pretty serious fly in the ointment.

ARGANTE: Don't you worry, I'll deal with it.

GERONTE: Children take a Hell of a lot of bringing up.

ARGANTE: Too bloody right. So?

GERONTE: So if they misbehave, the most likely explanation is that they've been *badly* brought up.

ARGANTE: What exactly are you driving at?

GERONTE: What exactly am I driving at?

ARGANTE: Hmm.

GERONTE: Well... only that this wouldn't have happened if you'd brought yor son up properly.

ARGANTE: I see. And of course you've brought yours up in exemplary fashion.

GERONTE: Certainly. And if he'd pulled a stunt like this I'd have given him what for, I can tell you.

ARGANTE: Oh really. And suppose he'd pulled an even worse one? Eh? What then? EH?

GERONTE: What?

ARGANTE: EHHHH?

GERONTE: What are you on about?

ARGANTE: You shouldn't be so quick to sneer at people. People with loads of shit on their own doorsteps shouldn't stand on other people's doorsteps sniffing.

GERONTE: I'm sorry?

ARGANTE: You know what I mean.

GERONTE: If you're implying... if you've heard something about my son...

ARGANTE: I might have.

GERONTE: What?

ARGANTE: Your man Scapin told me. He wasn't specific though. You'd better get the details from him. I'm off to consult a lawyer. (*Goes.*)

GERONTE: Pulled an even worse one? What even worse one? What *could* be worse? (*As LEANDRE enters.*) Ah! There you are.

LEANDRE: (*Running up to him to embrace him.*) Father! What a joy to have you back!

GERONTE: (*Dodging the embrace so that LEANDRE clasps the air.*) Steady!

LEANDRE: Don't you want a hug?

GERONTE: What have you pulled?

LEANDRE: Pardon?

GERONTE: You heard. What stunt have you pulled?

LEANDRE: You've lost me.

GERONTE: Look me in the eye.

LEANDRE: Papa...

GERONTE: LOOK ME IN THE EYE, BOY!

LEANDRE: All right...

GERONTE: What's been going on here? What have you done?

LEANDRE: I don't know. What am I *meant* to have done?

GERONTE: I wouldn't be asking if I knew, would I? What the pink blazes have you bloody *done*?

LEANDRE: Nothing bad.

GERONTE: Nothing bad?

LEANDRE: No.

GERONTE: You're sure?

LEANDRE: Absolutley.

GERONTE: According to Scapin...

LEANDRE: Scapin!

GERONTE: Aha! You've gone red.

LEANDRE: (*Wiping his face with his hand.*) What's he been saying? (*Under breath.*) The treacherous swine!

GERONTE: What was that?

LEANDRE: Nothing.

GERONTE: We should discuss this at home. I shall be going there directly. But if you've made a fool of me, I'll disown you. I will. I'll never see you or speak to you again. (*Goes.*)

LEANDRE: So Scapin's gone and given me away! He'll pay for this!

Enter SCAPIN and OCTAVE.

OCTAVE: Oh Scapin, how can I ever repay you? What a hero you are! Thank God you exist!

LEANDRE: Ah! There you are, you little... you little... (*Draws his sword.*) I'll teach you a lesson you won't forget!

SCAPIN: (*On his knees.*) Monsieur...

OCTAVE: (*Coming between them, to LEANDRE.*) Steady on!

LEANDRE: No, Octave, don't try and stop me.

SCAPIN: But monsieur...

OCTAVE: Léandre, for goodness' sake...

LEANDRE: (*Going to whack SCAPIN.*) I've got to get the anger out of me!

OCTAVE: Wait!

LEANDRE: No, Octave, he must confess his treachery. (*To SCAPIN.*) You see, I KNOW. I bet you thought you'd get away with it. Now I want to hear it from your lips. Go on, own up, or I'll run you through.

SCAPIN: Monsieur, you wouldn't have the heart. Would you?

LEANDRE: Come on, spit it out.

SCAPIN: What am I supposed to have done?

LEANDRE: You know damn well.

SCAPIN: I don't. I swear.

LEANDRE: (*Menacing him again.*) Oh no?

OCTAVE: (*Holding him back.*) Léandre!

SCAPIN: All right, I admit it – I drank that flagon of wine someone sent you the other day.

LEANDRE: That was you? I gave the maid a bollocking for that.

SCAPIN: I'm sorry, monsieur.

LEANDRE: Well it's not that.

SCAPIN: Not the wine?

LEANDRE: No. This is far more serious.

SCAPIN: What is it then?

LEANDRE: I want *you* to *tell* me.

SCAPIN: I don't remember anything else.

LEANDRE: (*Sword raised again.*) Then prepare to die!

SCAPIN: Hey!

OCTAVE: (*To LEANDRE, restraining him.*) For Heaven's sake, man!

SCAPIN: All right, monsieur, I admit it: remember you gave me that watch to give to your gipsy girl? And I came home covered in mud and blood and pretended I'd been beaten up and robbed? Well – I took it.

LEANDRE: *You Did What?!!*

SCAPIN: I took the watch. I wanted to know the time.

LEANDRE: Some servant you are! Well, it's not that either.

SCAPIN: It's not?

LEANDRE: No, you swine, it's something far worse.

SCAPIN: Oh!

LEANDRE: Now hurry up and spit it out.

SCAPIN: But that's all I've done, monsieur.

LEANDRE: Oh yes? (*Sword raised again.*)

SCAPIN: ALL RIGHT, then: remember you were attacked by a robber, and beaten to within an inch of your life, and fell down a hole while you were running away and nearly broke your neck?

LEANDRE: What about it?

SCAPIN: I was the robber.

LEANDRE: *You*?!

SCAPIN: Me. Sorry.

LEANDRE: Well I'll punish you for all that later. Now *what did you tell my Father?*

SCAPIN: Your father?

LEANDRE: Yes.

SCAPIN: I haven't even seen him since he got back.

LEANDRE: Oh no?

SCAPIN: Ask him.

LEANDRE: But he told me...

SCAPIN: Then he's lying – pardon my French.

Enter CARLE.

CARLE: The course of true love never did run smooth, Monsieur.

LEANDRE: Eh?

CARLE: Those gipsies are leaving, with your Zerbinetta. She told me to tell you, if you don't give them the money they're asking for by four o'clock today you'll lose her forever.

LEANDRE: By four o'clock?

CARLE: Yes.

LEANDRE: Scapin, you've got to help me!

SCAPIN: (*Immitating him.*) "Scapin, you've got to help me!" "Scapin you've got to help me!" *Ha* So now you need me all of a sudden.

LEANDRE: Get me the money and I'll overlook everything. And worse. If there is worse.

SCAPIN: No. No, you'd better run me through. In fact I want you to. Go on, kill me.

LEANDRE: I have no intention of killing you. I want *you* to save my life.

SCAPIN: No. You'd better get on with it. (*Beginning to bare his breast.*)

LEANDRE: You're too precious to me. You're infallible. A genius. I want that brilliant mind working for me now.

SCAPIN: Nope. Come on. Top me. (*His shirt is off.*)

LEANDRE: For God's sake Scapin, my happiness is in your hands.

OCTAVE: Yes, come on, Scapin.

SCAPIN: It's too late. He shouldn't have thrown a wobbly.

LEANDRE: Forget the wobbly, pleeeaase, and rescue me!

OCTAVE: Go on, Scapin.

SCAPIN: I shall *never* forget this affront.

OCTAVE: That's water under the bridge now.

LEANDRE: Scapin, will you abandon me in this crisis?

SCAPIN: Water under the bridge my arse!

LEANDRE: I was in the wrong. I admit it.

SCAPIN: You've insulted me.

LEANDRE: I'm really really sorry.

SCAPIN: He threatened to run me through.

LEANDRE: Please please please *please* I'm on my knees!

OCTAVE: There look.

SCAPIN: All right, get up. But don't be so hasty next time.

LEANDRE: So you will help?

SCAPIN: I'll think about it.

LEANDRE: We haven't got much time.

SCAPIN: Relax. How much do you need?

LEANDRE: Five hunrdred écus.

SCAPIN: (*To OCTAVE.*) And you?

OCTAVE: Two hundred pistoles.

SCAPIN: Fine. I'll get the money from your fathers. (*To OCTAVE.*) I already know how I'm going to trick yours. (*To LEANDRE.*) As for yours, well, he may be a miser, but he's also a complete idiot. He'll be easy. But here comes Octave's now. You'd better both go. (*To OCTAVE.*) Tell Silvestre to come quickly. It's time for him to play his part. (*OCTAVE goes with LEANDRE.*)

SCAPIN: (*Aside.*) He looks thoughtful.

ARGANTE: (*Thinks he's alone.*) What appalling behaviour! To throw himself into such an engagement. I don't know – young people nowadays!

SCAPIN: Your servant, monsieur.

ARGANTE: Hello, Scapin.

SCAPIN: Thinking about the business with your son?

ARGANTE: I'm furious about it.

SCAPIN: These things are sent to try us. We must always be prepared for the worst. As a philosopher once said...

ARGANTE: *What* did a philosopher once say?

SCAPIN: When a father goes away he should try and imagine all the terrible things that could happen while he's gone: his house burned down; his money stolen; his wife dead; his son crippled; his daughter deflowered; and count each thing that *doesn't* happen as a blessing. That's what I do. Whenever I go away I expect my master to be furious when I get back . I'm ready for anything – scoldings; insults; kicks up the arse; beatings – and I thank Heaven for whatever I don't get.

ARGANTE: Very sensible. But this marriage wrecks my plans. I won't have it. I've just seen a lawyer about getting it annulled.

SCAPIN: My god! I'd try something else, monsieur, if I were you. You know what a disaster a law-suit can be. It's like wandering into a thorny thicket.

ARGANTE: You're right. So what would you suggest?

SCAPIN: This might do the trick... I've been working something out, you see. It pissed me off to see you upset. I can't bear it when honest, decent fathers are messed about by their sons; it really gets my goat. And I'm particularly fond of *you*...

ARGANTE: How sweet.

SCAPIN: So I went to the girl's brother. One of those professional thugs, he is, all sword-thrusts and death-threats. Thinks no more of killing a man than cracking a nut. Well, we discussed the marriage. I pointed out how easily you could get it annulled, on grounds of force, not to mention your money and influence, your rights as a father, etc etc. Eventually I persuaded him and he agreed, for a sum of money...

ARGANTE: How much?

SCAPIN: A ludicrous amount at first.

ARGANTE: Yes?

SCAPIN: An incredible sum.

ARGANTE: Well?

SCAPIN: He was talking five or six hundred pistoles, minimum.

ARGANTE: *What the...*?!

SCAPIN: My very words. "What kind of an idiot do you take him for?" I said. We thrashed it out for a while, and then he said: "Look, I'm off to the army shortly. I have to get myself equipped and I'm strapped for cash. I'll settle for sixty pistoles, to buy a horse."

ARGANTE: He can have them.

SCAPIN: Then there's the harness and the guns.

ARGANTE: How much for them?

SCAPIN: Say another twenty.

ARGANTE: Twenty plus sixty makes eighty.

SCAPIN: Exactly right.

ARGANTE: Seems rather a lot but...

SCAPIN: "Then I'll need a nag for my servant," he said. That'll be another thirty pistoles."

ARGANTE: The servant can walk. The deal's off.

SCAPIN: Monsieur...

ARGANTE: Bloody cheek!

SCAPIN: You want the servant to walk?

ARGANTE: He can swim for all I care. And so can his master.

SCAPIN: Monsieur, don't spoil the ship for a ha'p'th of tar. Don't get into a law-suit, I beg of you. Suppose you lose? The *fees*. You'll be ruined.

ARGANTE: You're right. He can have the extra thirty.

SCAPIN: "Then I'm going to need a mule," he said, "to carry the..."

ARGANTE: I'll tell him where he can stick his mule. A law-suit it is.

SCAPIN: Please, monsieur...

ARGANTE: Nothing doing.

SCAPIN: But *monsieur*, just an itsy witsy little mule...

ARGANTE: I'll make him eat his sodding mule.

SCAPIN: But monsieur...

ARGANTE: No. I'd rather take them to court.

SCAPIN: But monsieur, think of it – the ins and outs; the ups and downs; all those bastards out to rip you off – advocates; sergeants; notaries; deputy public prosecutors; clerks; judges; *judges'* clerks... What do that lot care about justice? A sergeant'll trump up some charge or other and before you know it they'll convict you. Or your attorney'll strike a deal with your opponent and sell you down the river. He'll buy off your advocate too, so *he* won't turn up for the trial, or he'll deliberately come out with a lot of lousy arguments that lose the case. And if he *doesn't* appear the judge'll find against you by default. Or the recorder's clerk'll arrange for documents to disappear, or the recorder himself'll withold other evidence. Get the picture? You'll be shafted. The criminal justice system is Hell on earth. Do you want to go to Hell?

ARGANTE: *How* much for the mule?

SCAPIN: Monsieur, for the mule, the two horses, the harness, the guns, and something to give the woman he's billeted on, he wants a total of two hundred pistoles.

ARGANTE: Two hundred?

SCAPIN: Yes.

ARGANTE: (*Furious, pacing up and down.*) I'm taking it to court.

SCAPIN: You're not thinking.

ARGANTE: I bloody am.

SCAPIN: But you'll need money for a *lawsuit.* Money for writs. Money to get documents copied and checked and signed and sealed. Money for attorneys. Money for advocates. Money for counsel. Money for notaries. Money for your advocates' and your attorneys' attendance fees. Money for consultations and appeals and engrossing and deputy public prosecutors' reports and recordings and registrations and... and settlements out of court and settlements *in* court and settlements *after* court and more copying and checking and signing and sealing, to say nothing of bribes – bribes, bribes and more bribes. Give him the money.

ARGANTE: Two hundred pistoles?

SCAPIN: Yes. I've worked it out. It should come to at least a hundred and fifty less than a lawsuit. Not to mention all the trouble you'll save.

ARGANTE: Well I'm not giving him two hundred.

SCAPIN: Here he comes.

SILVESTRE: (*Entering, disguised as a "roaring boy".*) Scapin, this Argante fellow – Octave's father – I'd like to meet him, please.

SCAPIN: Why, monsieur?

SILVESTRE: I've just heard he wants to take me to court, to get my sister's marriage annulled.

SCAPIN: I'm not sure he does. But he doesn't like two hundred pistoles. He thinks it's too much.

SILVESTRE: By *thunder!* I'll skin 'im alive! Where is he?

ARGANTE hides behind SCAPIN.

SCAPIN: Monsieur, he's quite a man, he won't be scared of you.

SILVESTRE: Is that so? Ecod! I'll flay 'im, I'll skewer 'im! Where is 'e? I'll rip 'is guts out and use 'em as a belt! Od's kittikins! Who's that?

SCAPIN: Not him!

SILVESTRE: Friend of his, is 'e?

SCAPIN: No, monsieur, as a matter of fact he's his worst enemy.

SILVESTRE: Really?

SCAPIN: Yes.

SILVESTRE: Excellent. (*To ARGANTE.*) So you're that turd Argante's arch-enemy, eh?

ARGANTE is speechless with fear.

SCAPIN: I'll vouch for him.

SILVESTRE: (*Grabbing ARGANTE's hand.*) Put it there. I swear to you, on my honour, by this sword, by all the oaths under the sun, that before this day is done I shall rid you of this poltroon, this ponce, this fuckwit of an Argante. You may depend on me.

SCAPIN: Monsieur, no violence, please!

SILVESTRE: What do you mean, no violence? 'Zounds, I'll... I'll... I'll...

SCAPIN: He'll fight his corner, sir. He has friends, he has family, he has servants to defend him.

SILVESTRE: Good. The more the merrier. (*He draws his sword and starts thrusting wildly in all directions at imaginary enemies*.) 'sblood! Egad! Gadzooks! I'm ready for 'em. The whole pack of 'em. Thirty of 'em. Swords drawn. Pish! Tush! I ask no quarter, I give no quarter. Have at ye, varlets! Where are they? Take that! And that! And that! (*Still thrusting.*)

SCAPIN: Hey! Monsieur! It's not us!

SILVESTRE: *I'll* see to 'em! *I'll* sort 'em out! (*Exit thrusting.*)

SCAPIN: We're all going to die, for two hundred pistoles. Tragic.

ARGANTE: (*Trembling.*) Scapin...

SCAPIN: Yes?

ARGANTE: Perhaps I should give him the money.

SCAPIN: Phew!

ARGANTE: Go and find him. I've got two hundred on me.

SCAPIN: Just give them to me. *You* can't give them to him, on a point of honour... not now you've passed yourself off as someone else. Besides, he might ask you for more.

ARGANTE: I'd rather give my money to people in person.

SCAPIN: Don't you trust me?

ARGANTE: It's not that, but...

SCAPIN: I'm either honest or *dis*honest; one or the other. Why would I cheat you? Who am I working for here? You and my master, whose daughter your son is marrying. If you don't trust me I wash my hands of the whole business. You'll have to find someone else to sort it out for you.

ARGANTE: Hey! Wait!

SCAPIN: Nope. I wouldn't trust me if I were you. I'm bound to run off with your pistoles.

ARGANTE: Wait, I tell you! You must go, but for God's sake be careful.

SCAPIN: Leave everything to me.

ARGANTE: I'll wait for you at my house.

SCAPIN: I'll see you there. (*Alone, licks his finger "one to me".*) Now for the other numbskull. Talk of the devil! Into the trap they walk, one after the other. (*As GERONTE enters.*) Oh, God, oh, God, oh God! The shame! The disgrace! Oh, the poor father! Poor old Géronte! What's he going to *do*?

GERONTE: What's he saying about me? Why does he look so sad?

SCAPIN: Where is he? Where's poor Géronte?

GERONTE: Scapin? What's the matter?

SCAPIN: I have to tell him this terrible news.

GERONTE: What's happened?

SCAPIN: I've been hunting high and low for him.

GERONTE: Here I am.

SCAPIN: I wonder where he's hiding.

GERONTE: Are you blind? Here I am, look.

SCAPIN: Ah! Monsieur. Your son...

GERONTE: What about him?

SCAPIN: He's in terrible trouble.

GERONTE: Go on.

SCAPIN: I was with him just now. He seemed very upset. You'd said something. About me. I wanted to take his mind off it, so I went for a stroll with him down to the port. We saw an Arab ship there. Splendid it was.

A handsome young Arab invited us aboard. He was incredibly polite; gave us lunch; wonderful fruit; fantastic wine...

GERONTE: What's so terrible about all that?

SCAPIN: I'm coming to the bad part. While we were eating and drinking he put out to sea! Then he sent me back in a rowing boat to tell you that, if you don't send him five hundred écus at once, he's going to take Léandre off to Algeria.

GERONTE: What the...?! Five hundred écus?!

SCAPIN: Yes, monsieur. He gave me two hours.

GERONTE: Filthy Arab bastard! Tell him I'm going to get the law onto him.

SCAPIN: Oh, come on! On the open sea?

GERONTE: Why the Hell did he go aboard?

SCAPIN: Bad luck I suppose.

GERONTE: Scapin, the time has come for you to prove your worth.

SCAPIN: How?

GERONTE: You're to take a boat and go after this Arab and tell him to return my son. You must take Léandre's place till I've raised the money.

SCAPIN: You're mad, monsieur! What would the Arab want with *me*?

GERONTE: Why in God's name did he go *aboard?*

SCAPIN: How could he guess what was going to happen? Remember, though – we've only got two hours.

GERONTE: And where am I supposed to find five hundred écus in two hours?

SCAPIN: You're going to have to try.

GERONTE: Here's the key to my strong room.

SCAPIN: Good.

GERONTE: Open it.

SCAPIN: Yes.

GERONTE: You'll find a big key on a shelf to the left. It opens the door to the attic.

SCAPIN: Yes.

GERONTE: You'll find a big basket full of clothes up there. Take them to a second-hand clothes shop and see what you can get for them.

SCAPIN: You *are* mad. I won't get a hundred francs for that lot. Besides, it'll take more than two hours to sell them.

GERONTE: Why the Devil did he...?

SCAPIN: Who knows, but he did. And you'll lose him if you don't hurry.

GERONTE: I'll find the money.

SCAPIN: You'd better be quick about it.

GERONTE: Four hundred écus, you said...?

SCAPIN: *Five* hundred.

GERONTE: Why the...?

SCAPIN: Look, there's not a moment to lose.

GERONTE: As a matter of fact I've got five hundred on me. (*Reluctantly he produces his purse; he swings his arm from side to side; SCAPIN makes repeated corresponding grabs at the purse and finally gets it.*) There you are then. Go and pay the ransom.

SCAPIN: Right you are.

GERONTE: But tell the Arab he's a shit from me.

SCAPIN: Will do.

GERONTE: An unadulterated turd.

SCAPIN: Fine.

GERONTE: A nasty, swindling swine.

SCAPIN: Got it.

Exit GERONTE, enter OCTAVE and LEANDRE.

SCAPIN: The five hundred really hurts. But I haven't finished with him yet. Not after what he told monsieur Léandre.

OCTAVE: Well, Scapin? Did you get my money?

LEANDRE: And mine?

SCAPIN: Here you are: two hundred pistoles.

OCTAVE: You hero!

SCAPIN: (*To LEANDRE.*) Nothing doing for *you*, I'm afraid.

LEANDRE: (*Going.*) Then I'm going to hang myself. Life's not worth living without Zerbinetta.

SCAPIN: Hey! Hang on! I've got it here.

LEANDRE: Oh Scapin, you miracle-worker!

SCAPIN: On condition that you let me have my revenge on your father, for telling you whatever he told you.

LEANDRE: You have my permission.

SCAPIN: Monsieur Octave's my witness.

LEANDRE: Fine.

SCAPIN: All right, here you are: five hundred écus.

LEANDRE: Come on, let's go and buy my darling girl.

End of Act Two.

ACT THREE

SILVESTRE, SCAPIN, HYACINTE, ZERBINETTA.

SILVESTRE: Yup, it's all sorted.

SCAPIN: (*To ZERBINETTA.*) Do you love my master with all your heart?

ZERBINETTA: I'm not sure yet. Hearts can't be bought, you know. Is he going to *marry* me?

SCAPIN: Yes. His intentions are entirely honourable. I wouldn't have got involved if they weren't.

ZERBINETTA: I dare say. But what about his father?

SCAPIN: We can handle him.

HYACINTE: We're in the same boat, you and I.

ZERBINETTA: But *you* have a family. What father wants a daughter-in-law with no connections? Money is so important in these matters.

HYACINTE: But *your* lover isn't marrying someone else.

ZERBINETTA: The real problem is always the father.

HYACINTE: Obstacles, obstacles, why must there always be obstacles?

SCAPIN: There have to be downs in life is well as ups. Who was it said:

> "Without an obstacle or two to beat
> Happiness can never be complete"?

Now, if you'll excuse me, I've got a score to settle.

SILVESTRE: You're risking a beating.

SCAPIN: Risk is the spice of life. Who was it said...?

SILVESTRE: It's your arse on the line.

SCAPIN: I can take it.

ZERBINETTA: We'll be needing you soon.

SCAPIN: I'll be with you shortly.

(*The others go; GERONTE enters.*)

GERONTE: Well, Scapin, have you got my son back?

SCAPIN: He's safe. But you're not.

GERONTE: Why?

SCAPIN: He's looking for you. He wants to kill you.

GERONTE: Me?

SCAPIN: Yes.

GERONTE: Who does?

SCAPIN: The brother of the girl Octave has married. He thinks the marriage is being annulled because you're trying to get your daughter married to Octave. So he's decided to kill you. On a point of honour. He's got a lot of friends out looking for you. Really nasty pieces of work they are. Swashbuckling types like him. You can't go home – they're lying in wait for you.

GERONTE: What shall I do?

SCAPIN: Search me. Hang on... (*Pretends to have heard someone and goes off, rear to look; comes back.*) False alarm.

GERONTE: Scapin, you've got to save me.

SCAPIN: I can't. Leastways, not without risking my *own* neck.

GERONTE: For pity's sake, don't desert me in my hour of need!

SCAPIN: I won't, monsieur. You see, I'm fond of you.

GERONTE: You'll be well rewarded. You can have this coat when I've finished with it.

SCAPIN: You're too generous. Now: get into this sack, and whatever you do, *keep absolutely still.* I'm going to carry you on my back, you see? Like some sort of bundle. That way I can smuggle you home. Then we'll get hold of some guns and barricade ourselves in.

GERONTE: Brilliant!

SCAPIN: Glad you approve. (*Under breath.*) Stupid old jerk! I'll teach you!

GERONTE: What was that?

SCAPIN: I said it's bound to work. Now, get right in, well hidden, and whatever happens don't move or make a sound.

GERONTE: (*Popping his head out.*) Don't worry, I won't.

SCAPIN: Get your head back in! Here comes one of them now. He's looking for you. (*Putting on a voice.*) "Where's that senile old sod, GERONTE? I want to kill him." (*Whispering to GERONTE in his own voice.*) Don't say *anything.* (*Back to false voice.*) "I'll find him wherever he is." (*Own voice, whisper.*) Keep hidden. (*False voice.*) "Aha! A man carrying a sack!" Good day, monsieur. "I'll give you a louis if you tell me where Géronte is." You're looking for monsieur Géronte? "Yes." What for? "What for?" Yes. "I want to thrash him to death." You can't do that to *him.* "Why not? He's a nasty old git; a snivelling old shit." A nasty old git? A snivelling old shit? How *dare* you? "Friend of his are you?" Yes, monsieur, I am. "I see! Then take that for him, from me, and that, and that." (*Thumping the sack with a stick.*) Hey! Stop! (*More thwacks.*) "Be sure to pass those on. Good day to you."

GERONTE: (*Popping his head out of the sack.*) Oh god! Scapin, I can't go on with this.

SCAPIN: I'm in agony.

GERONTE: *You're* in agony?!

SCAPIN: Sshh! Here comes another one. "Where the Hell is that old bastard Géronte?" Keep your head in! "Hey, you: I'm looking for an old bastard called Géronte. Have you seen him?" No, monsieur. "I want the truth, mind. I've got some business with him. Nothing important. I just want to smash his skull and rip his guts out." I swear to you, I don't know where he is. "What have you got in that sack? It saw it move just then." I'm sorry? "There's something or someone in that sack." No there isn't. "We'll soon see. I'm going to stick my sword into it." Don't do that, monsieur! "Show me what you've got in it then." Mind your own business. "*Show me! Right now.*" It's just a bundle of old clothes. "Then let's have a look." No! "I'll thwack you with this stick..." Go ahead! "All right, you asked for it!" (*Same business as before.*) Ow! Ayo! Ayeee! "That'll teach you to mess me about! Goodbye... *for now...*"

GERONTE: (*Popping his head out of the sack.*) He nearly killed me!

SCAPIN: Me too! Look out! Here comes a whole bunch of them. (*Pretends to be several thugs.*) "We've got to find him. – Search high and low. – Look in every nook and cranny. – What about over there? – No, here. – Left. – No, right. – No, here." Keep well hidden. "Look, lads, there's his servant. Hey! You! Where's your master?" Please don't hurt me! "Tell us where he is! Come on! Quick! We haven't got all day." Steady on, gentlemen! (*GERONTE eases his head out of the sack and sees what SCAPIN is up to.*) "Fetch your master this minute or we'll break every bone in your body." Go on then. I'm not telling you where he is. "We'll kill you..." Go ahead! "All right, you asked for it..." *No!* (*He's about to deliver a thwack when GERONTE leaps out of the sack.*)

GERONTE: *Why, you little...!*

SCAPIN runs off. Enter ZERBINETTA laughing.

GERONTE: (*Not seeing her.*) I swear to God I'll make him pay for this.

ZERBINETTA: I can't get over it! What a hilarious business! What a *gullible* old idiot! Ha ha ha!

GERONTE: It's not funny.

ZERBINETTA: I'm sorry?

GERONTE: It's no joke.

ZERBINETTA: What are you talking about?

GERONTE: Why were you laughing at me?

ZERBINETTA: I wasn't. Someone just told me something hilarious. At any rate, *I* think it's hilarious. But then I'm mixed up in it. A young man just swindled some money out of his father.

GERONTE: You interest me strangely.

ZERBINETTA: It's a hoot. Want to hear?

GERONTE: Please.

ZERBINETTA: I suppose it's all right to tell you. It's bound to get out soon. I'm a gypsy. You know – wandering from place to place, telling fortunes, and so on. Well, shortly after I arrived in Naples a young man saw me and fell in love with me. He's been pursuing me ever since. All young men are alike. They think they've only got to say the word and you're theirs for the taking. But he had to think again. He told my guardians that he loved me, and they said he could have me, *provided* he paid them some money. The trouble was that, as is often the case with young men, my sweetheart was a bit strapped for cash. What's more his father's not only rich but a total skinflint. A really mean old monster, by the sound of it. Now what was his name? Maybe you know him. Met any mean old monsters in this town?

GERONTE: No.

ZERBINETTA: It ends in "ron" or "ronte" or some such. Or... Oronte... no... Gér... Géronte – that's it! that's him! The stupid old prat, the miserable old snurge! Now, here's what it boils down to: my people have decided to leave Naples today. My sweetypie was going to lose me because he couldn't get hold of the money. But in the nick of time he was rescued by his servant, who managed to con it out of his father. That servant's a genius. A real wizard. His name's Scapin.

GERONTE: (*Aside.*) The treacherous little...

ZERBINETTA: I'll tell you how he did it shall I? (*Laughing.*) Just thinking about it makes me roar. (*Laughing.*) He told this Géronte that he and his son had gone on board an Arab ship, and a young man had given them a meal, and while they were eating the ship had put to sea, and the Arab had sent him back in a boat to tell his master's father that the Arab was going to take his son off to Algeria, if he didn't send him five hundred écus at once. (*Laughing.*) Well, the old moron had a fit over this. His love for his son was fighting with his love for his money. Being asked for five hundred écus was like being stabbed five hundred times through the heart. (*Laughing.*) He suggested various alternatives. The servant vetoed all of them. "Why the Hell did he go aboard" the old buffoon kept saying.

"Why in God's name did he go aboard!" Eventually, after much moaning and groaning... But you don't seem to find this funny.

GERONTE: I think this young man's a total bastard. And I'm sure his father'll thrash him to within an inch of his life when he gets hold of him. And *you've* no business referring to a respectable man as a "stupid old prat". He'll teach you to come here and seduce people's sons. As for the servant, by Christ!, I'll... monsieur Géronte'll see him swing for this! (*Goes.*)

Enter SILVESTRE.

SILVESTRE: Where the Hell have you been? You realise who you were talking to just then? Only monsieur Léandre's father!

ZERBINETTA: What? Not old Géronte himself! Oh dear! No wonder he wasn't amused. And I've gone and told him the whole story!

SILVESTRE: You did *what*!

ZERBINETTA: I was dying to share it with somebody. I dont suppose it much matters.

SILVESTRE: You're a bloody idiot!

ZERBINETTA: He'd have heard it from someone else – wouldn't he?

Enter ARGANTE.

ARGANTE: Silvestre!

SILVESTRE: (*To ZERBINETTA.*) Go back inside. My master's calling me.

ARGANTE: So you were in cahoots, eh – you and Scapin and my son! You were out to swindle me, and you thought I'd take it lying down.

SILVESTRE: Scapin may have been out to swindle you, monsieur. I don't know anything about it.

ARGANTE: We'll see, you... you... you... No one's going to get the better of *me*.

Enter GERONTE.

GERONTE: Argante, I feel such a *fool*!

ARGANTE: Ditto.

GERONTE: That bastard Scapin's cheated me out of five hundred écus.

ARGANTE: Bastard is right.

GERONTE: You too? How much?

ARGANTE: Two hundred pistoles.

GERONTE: He's made a total ass of me. He'll live to regret it.

ARGANTE: You bet he will.

SILVESTRE: (*Aside.*) *Uh*-oh!

GERONTE: To make matters worse, it looks as though my daughter may have drowned. She should have got here from Tarentum by now.

ARGANTE: Why was she in Tarentum anyway?

GERONTE: That's another story. I had to keep my second marriage a secret, for various reasons. What's this? Her nurse! (*Enter NERINE.*) Nérine?

NERINE: Monsieur Pandolphe...

GÉRONTE: No need to call me that now. I only used that name when we were all in Tarentum. Call me Géronte.

NERINE: No wonder we couldn't find you. Goodness! we've had a rare old time of it!

GERONTE: My daughter, and her mother, where are they?

NERINE: Your daughter's nearby. But first of all I have to tell you... er... um... she's married. You see, what with not being able to find you, and all the chaos...

GERONTE: MARRIED!!!!!!!!!

NERINE: Yes.

GERONTE: Who to?

NERINE: Someone called Octave. Son of someone called Argante.

GERONTE and ARGANTE: (*Together.*) *My god!... My god!... My god!*

GERONTE: Where is she? Take us to her! NOW!

NERINE: She's just in there – in that house.

GERONTE: Come on, Argante! (*They go.*)

SILVESTRE: Well I'll be jiggered!

Enter SCAPIN.

SCAPIN: Silvestre, what's going on?

SILVESTRE: Well, Octave's in the clear. Who do you suppose Hyacinte is? Only monsieur Géronte's daughter! So both the old codgers are happy. They're probably going to kill *you*, though, or at any rate thrash you. I should steer especially clear of monsieur Géronte, if I were you.

SCAPIN: Ah, shucks, who gives a toss? It's all just empty threats.

SILVESTRE: I'd watch your back. The sons and the fathers'll make peace, leaving *you* out on a limb; and a pretty shaky limb at that.

SCAPIN: Don't you worry about me. I'll make my peace with them somehow.

SILVESTRE: They're coming back out.

SCAPIN scuttles off as GERONTE, ARGANTE, NERINE and HYACINTE come out of the house.

GERONTE: Come along, my darling. Ah, if only your mother were with you, my happiness would be complete.

Enter OCTAVE and ZERBINETTA.

ARGANTE: Come along, my boy. This is a very happy day. It's time to celebrate your marriage! Yes, Heaven has...

OCTAVE: (*Not noticing HYACINTE.*) No, father, it's out of the question. I have to come clean with you now. You've heard about my...

ARGANTE: Yes, but you don't know...

OCTAVE: I know all I need to know.

ARGANTE: No, you see, monsieur Géronte's daughter...

OCTAVE: I'll never care two hoots for *her.*

GERONTE: But she's the...

OCTAVE: It's no good, monsieur Géronte, my affections are engaged else...

SILVESTRE: Listen...

OCTAVE: No.

ARGANTE: Your wife...

OCTAVE: No, father, I can't give Hyacinte up. I'd rather die. Ah! There she *is!* (*He crosses over to her.*) I'm hers and only hers, till death do us part.

ARGANTE: That's just as well, since she's the one we want you to marry! You had to make a stand though, didn't you, you little twerp!

HYACINTE: Octave, this is my long-lost father. Our troubles are over.

GERONTE: Let's go to my house. We can talk about it there.

HYACINTE: Father, you see this adorable creature here? Please don't part me from her.

GERONTE: Your brother was betrothed to her, and he never asked my permission. What's more she's just been extremely rude about me, to my face.

ZERBINETTA: Monsieur, please forgive me. I wouldn't have said such things if I'd known who you were. I only knew you by repute, you see.

GERONTE: What do you mean, repute?

HYACINTE: Father, they've done nothing wrong. I can vouch for her. She's a decent, respectable girl.

GERONTE: Oh, wonderful. So I'm supposed to let my son marry a girl no one knows anything about? A vagabond? A gypsy?

Enter LEANDRE.

LEANDRE: She *is* a vagabond, it's true. She may have no exalted connections; no fortune; but the gypsies I've just purchased her from assured me that her people are entirely respectable. It seems the gypsies in question kidnapped her when she was four. Look: here's a bracelet they gave me, which will help you find out who her parents are.

ARGANTE: Good Heavens! Not *that* bracelet! Why, this is my long lost daughter, who disappeared when she was four years old!

GERONTE: Your daughter?

ARGANTE: Yes. It's her all right. She looks just like her mother.

HYACINTE: Well, I never! What an amazing day it's been!

Enter CARLE.

CARLE: You'll never guess what's happened!

GERONTE: What?

CARLE: Poor old Scapin...

GERONTE: *Ha! Him!* I'll see him hang.

CARLE: No need, monsieur. He was walking down the street just now, and a block of masonry fell on his head. Bashed half his brains out. They're bringing him here now. He wants to speak to you before he dies.

ARGANTE: Where is he?

CARLE: Here.

Enter SCAPIN, carried on by two men, his head bandaged, as though it's been cracked open.

SCAPIN: Ahhh!!... Here I am, gentlemen... and not in a very good way, I'm afraid... Ahi!... I had to ask your forgiveness before I... before I... before I *went*... Ohhh!... If I've done wrong, I beg you to forgive me... Aaaaaaaa!... Especially you, monsieur Argante... and you, monsieur Géronte... Hmmmrrrgggh!

ARGANTE: You're forgiven. Die in peace.

SCAPIN: (*To GERONTE.*) You were the one I wronged the most, monsieur... what with the sack and the beatings...

GERONTE: Forget it.

SCAPIN: But it was outrageous of me; I mean, to actually take a stick to...

GERONTE: Please, Scapin...

SCAPIN: It's no use, I can't forgive *myself.*

GERONTE: For Heaven's sake, man, shut up about it!

SCAPIN: What was I thinking of? To hit my own master with a...

GERONTE: *I said: Shut up about it!!*

SCAPIN: You're too good to me. But do you really...?

GERONTE: *Yes*, for Christ's sake, I *forgive* you! Now can we please drop it?

SCAPIN: Oh, sir, you've taken such a *weight* off my mind.

GERONTE: Fine. Of course, you're only forgiven on condition that you die.

SCAPIN: Eh?

GERONTE: If you survive, you're for it.

SCAPIN: Oh! Oh! Another brain spasm! Ah!

ARGANTE: You know, I think we should forgive him regardless, since everything's turned out so well.

GERONTE: Oh, all right then.

ARGANTE: Now let's go and have supper. We've got a lot of celebrating to do.

SCAPIN: You'd better put me at the end of the table, in case I *do* die.

THE END.